WITH
☞ W9-AYP-452

Saints at Your Service

The 10 worst things:
To long for something that comes not
To lie in bed and sleep not
To work hard and please not
To have a vehicle that goes not
To employ a person who obeys not
To be loveless and hope not
To be sick and recover not
To lose one's way and know it not
To knock at a door and enter not
To have a friend you trust not
——Traditional proverb

If you're suffering from even one of these conditions, take heart: A patron saint exists who *really* wants to help you. Curious? See if you can match the following saints with their celestial specialities:

1. St. Wilgefortis
2. St. Martin de Porres
3. St. Joan of Arc
4. St. Apollonia
5. St. Joseph
6. St. Michael the Archangel
7. Mother Cabrini
8. St. Basil the Great

a. Invoked against crime and vandalism
b. Patron of sick animals
c. Solves your transportation woes
d. Discourages unwanted lovers
e. Patron of cross-dressers
f. The best Realtor you'll ever find
g. A lawyer with no billable hours
h. Relieves your toothache without Novocain

Learn about these and other celestial helpers in *Heaven Help Us*
Answers: 1, d; 2, b; 3, e; 4, h; 5, f; 6, a; 7, c; 8, g.

Heaven Help Us

The Worrier's Guide to the Patron Saints

Alice La Plante and Clare La Plante

A Dell Trade Paperback

A DELL TRADE PAPERBACK

Published by
Dell Publishing
a division of
Random House, Inc.
1540 Broadway
New York, New York 10036

Copyright © 1999 by Alice La Plante and Clare La Plante

All rights reserved. No part of this book may be reproduced or transmitted in any form or by any means, electronic or mechanical, including photocopying, recording, or by any information storage and retrieval system, without the written permission of the Publisher, except where permitted by law.

Dell books may be purchased for business or promotional use or for special sales. For information please write to: Special Markets Department. Random House, Inc., 1540 Broadway, New York, N.Y. 10036.

DTP and the colophon are trademarks of Random House, Inc.

Library of Congress Cataloging in Publication Data
La Plante, Alice.
      Heaven help us : the worrier's guide to the patron saints / Alice La Plante & Clare La Plante.
          p.   cm.
      Includes index.
      ISBN 0-440-50865-7 (pbk.)
      1. Christian patron saints Biography.   I. La Plante, Clare.
II. Title.
BX4656.5.L36 1999   99-24176
282'.092'2—dc21   CIP
[B]

Printed in the United States of America

Published simultaneously in Canada
Book design by Michele Wetherbee
Book illustrations © Timothy Basil Ering
November 1999
10 9 8 7 6 5 4
CWO
ISBN-13: 978-0-440-50865-6

We dedicate this book to our parents,

Dr. William La Plante

and Alice O'Neill La Plante

Acknowledgments

*I*t would take far too much space here to personally thank everyone who helped us with this book.
But we wanted to express our special gratitude to the
following people:

First, we'd like to thank our brillant agent, Arielle
Eckstut of James Levine Communications, for her
enthusiasm, vision, and—can we say?—discernment.
We found her help indispensable and her guidance
inspiring. We'd also like to extend our warm gratitude
to our editor at Dell Publishing, Kathleen Jayes,
whose patience, humor, and editorial wisdom provided the supportive environment that allowed the
creative team to flourish. Timothy Basil Ering's illustrations are the work of an angel, and Michele
Wetherbee achieved a design perfectly aligned with
our vision.

Special thanks are also owed to Sister Ann
Edward Bennis, SSJ; Marion Bergan; Sister Maura
Lowrey, RSM; Sister Joan Rice, RA; Sister Virginia
Thoennes, SLW; Father Edward Hays; Jenny Yetsky;
and Mary Alice Fedor, all of whom provided invalu-
able contributions in the form of patron saint lore.
To Rick Trushel of Absolutely Books (abbooks
@best.com), who went to heroic lengths to track down
rare and out-of-print publications. To Victoria
Rebeck, Susan Lally, Florence Merkl; Victoria Lui;
Patricia Leninger; Jeanette Hecker, Sonny Ginsberg,
Rich Seidner, Sarah Seidner, Rosalba Lopez, Nancy
Groth, Heather Donovan, Michelle Carter, and Jill
Simonsen, all of whom provided all-important emo-

tional and/or technical support during the researching and writing of this book. And, finally, to Tom Siedell and Alice O'Neill La Plante, our resident theological experts, who generously read the manuscript for errors. (Any remaining gaffes, however, are, of course, our own responsibility.)

Contents

Prologue: Why We Wrote This Book   1

What Is a Saint, Anyway? (And Why   3
Would You Ask One to Help You?)

The Sacred and the Profane   8

How a Saint Is Made: An Illustration   14

When Love's Labors Lose   17
Calling on Heaven's Cupids

Coping with Anxiety   43
Let the True Experts Help You Achieve
Spiritual Tranquillity

Missing Objects   69
Sending Out a Saint A.P.B.

School Stress   77
When a Little Learning Is a Dangerous Thing

Heavenly House Calls   85
A Truly Holistic Approach to Good Health

Guarding the Hearth and Home   123
Activating Your Own Spiritual Security
System

For Wandering Souls   145
Travel Insurance for an Increasingly
Mobile Planet

Miscellaneous Helpers   157
And Jacks-of-all-Trades in Spiritual
Intercession

Prayers   194

Index of Patronages Assigned to Saints   201

A Select Bibliography   207

Index   209

HEAVEN HELP US

Prologue:
Why We Wrote This Book

We (the authors of this book) are sisters. Two women who come from a family of worriers. A large Catholic family of worriers. Relying on the patron saints as antidotes to this worry was bred into us from the moment of the first emergency-room visit to that first . . . whatever. Saint Jude? Patron of hopeless causes? You were certainly needed (and often called upon).

And say we lost something. A younger sibling, let's say. We used Saint Antony, just as others relied on more traditional lost and found departments or bureaus of missing persons. Along with the title of our first cars, we were given Saint Christopher medals for our visors—even though that saint had long been dethroned. And like everyone else who grew up in Chicago, we knew Saint Joseph was the most reliable Realtor you could employ.

Despite all this, we realized recently—as we took on more adult responsibilities of jobs, families, homes—that our repertoire of patron saint rituals and prayers (the things we could actually *do* or *say*) was worryingly small.

True, hundreds of books on saints exist. Biographies, children's books, dictionaries, theological tomes. But although many of these books contain indexes listing the various patron saints—and some even include prayers—none offer a truly practical guide. Yes, you might be able to find that Saint Lucy is the patron saint of eye ailments—that's useful. But none will tell you what you can do or say to get the intercessionary help. Not that we doubt that Saint Joseph or Anne will listen to and act upon a heartfelt plea, but rituals are calming in and of themselves. Chants, repetitive prayers, ceremonies—humans have created and used these over the centuries for good reason.

So we decided to write a book that would be the indispensable reference guide for worriers such as ourselves. To offer a compilation of saint folklore and tradition for those irrational terrors that are terrible precisely because logic is too puny a weapon to use against them.

And here's an interesting footnote: Our first title was *The Insomniac's Guide to the Patron Saints,* for the simple reason that we happened to do our most intense worrying in the wee hours of the morning. However, when our agent told us that she, too, worried, but was a dedicated somniac, we decided to give our project an equal opportunity title. Worriers of the world, unite!

Over the course of several years we collected rituals and prayers from all over the country—and all over the world. Prayers and rituals that have been around for centuries. Time tested. Robust. Created from the real-life struggles of real people throughout the ages.

Read on. See for yourself.

What Is a Saint, Anyway?
(And Why Would You Ask One
to Help You?)

It's not as simple a question as you might think.

In our secular vocabulary, the word "saint" has come to mean an exceptionally good person. We often call people "saints" as a way of showing our respect and admiration. There is also often the implication that the person has undergone significant hardship—either in the pursuit of doing good or as the result of coping with a difficult situation. Consult your thesaurus and you'll find such synonyms as "sufferer," "martyr," "scapegoat," and "victim."

Still, using the word to describe a living person is, strictly speaking, incorrect. Only the deceased can legitimately be called saints. And here's a little-understood point: Officially, according to Roman Catholic theology, a saint is any soul who resides in heaven. To put it plainly, that's anyone who has died and who has not gone to hell. Souls in purgatory (in Latin, that's literally "the place of purging") are guaranteed to eventually become saints—as soon as they suffer enough to be considered purified of all earthly sins.

So all souls in heaven are saints. Yet to use the title of "Saint" before someone's name (as in Saint John or Saint Elizabeth) is another matter altogether. That's reserved for an elite group of heavenly residents.

The American Heritage Dictionary of the English Language defines a saint as a "person officially recognized by the Roman Catholic Church and certain other Christian churches as being entitled to public veneration."

Of course, sainthood wasn't always officially sanctioned. From the beginning of time as we know it the faithful have flocked to the extraordinary faithful, wanting to follow them, live as they did, even be buried by their graves.

In fact, saints used to be created by popular consensus. Saints were those people who had earned the respect and admiration of their local communities and who were honored after their deaths by the people who knew them best. But this way of creating saints began to get out of hand in the Middle Ages when the numbers of those designated saints by the faithful grew to unmanageable proportions. The Church finally stepped in—to add objectivity and to prevent saints from being adored (adoration is due to God alone).

The Church soon decreed that only it could decide who was worthy of being called saint. Still, the large majority of saints, and indeed many of the best known, were designated in the Church's first century before the official Vatican canonization process began around the year 200.

Perhaps because there were so many first-century saints made popular by concensus, without any official "fact-finding" committees appointed or formal criteria to fulfill, much of saints history turns out to be a fascinating mixture of fact and legend. There were few, if any, written records. As this book will show, the facts of the lives of the saints have often been blurred by the needs, passions, and politics of the times in which they lived. Also, prior pagan beliefs and legends became inextricably mixed with Christian theology as it slowly spread across the globe.

That is why a large number of so-called saints were ... let's say unseated ... by the Catholic Church in 1969. Church officials decided there was little evidence (or, in some cases, none at all) that the saints in question had ever existed. For impressionable young Catholics, this was a traumatic time. The very popular Saint Christopher was among the saints exposed as fraudulent. Historically the patron saint of wayfarers, he is now used to ensure safe journeys by car. (Check for yourself how many cars still have Saint Christopher medals hanging from rearview mirrors or Saint Christopher statues attached to dashboards, despite the fact that Saint Christopher has officially been declared *sanctus* non grata.)

So who are the official saints? Martyrs are automatic saints. (The Church used to distinguish between "red" martyrs—those who actually died for their faith—and "white"—those who merely suffered.) Otherwise a saint needs an impressive dossier (to be checked over carefully by the Vatican's Congregation for the Causes for Saints) and at least two miracles (to be attributed to that individual after his or her death). Mary is the chief saint. Angels (such as Gabriel) are also saints.

There's an important distinction to be made here: Catholics don't pray to saints, they pray *with* them. And, of course, you don't need to be Catholic to enlist their help: saints are defined less by the religious beliefs of those in need than by the fact that a supplicant requires aid.

Saints exist who have a specific interest in you. Any saint who has been honored on your birthday. Any saint who shares your name. Patron saints are also active on your behalf according to country, ethnicity, and vocation. And saints specialize in human dilemmas. They can help you find your lost glasses, your dream house, your soul mate. They can be invoked against illness, pests, and twitching.

So saints are our heavenly helpers. They assist us in our careers, in our personal endeavors, and especially in our struggles. Each day of the calendar year has at least one patron saint. Some have several (a saint's feast day is usually the day he or she died). New saints are constantly being "made." The current Pope, John Paul II, has streamlined the process by reducing the number of miracles required from four to two and getting rid of the "Devil's Advocate," someone the Vatican appoints to find holes in the saint's case. He's also canonized over two hundred saints and beatified (the first step on the sainthood journey) over seven hundred—more than any other pope in history.

We're moving back toward the original notion of saints as local beacons of spiritual strength, as people who lived lives that were ordinary in many ways. Many of the new saints being made today are not known beyond their small village or geographic region. Perhaps most significantly, this reminds us that someone doesn't have to be famous or powerful to qualify for sainthood. That saints don't have to make the cover of *People* or win a prestigious humanitarian award.

So the tradition of appealing to the saints for help with everyday problems has come full circle. We're increasingly reminded that they actually lived—often in nonsaintly ways—here on earth. That they suffered the slings and arrows of outrageous fortune (sometimes literally) just as we do. That we should think of them as trusted friends or family members— all right, so maybe a very intense friend or family member—but still, the kind of people we'd feel comfortable calling at 3:00 a.m. for comfort, knowing we'll always get good advice and that we'll never be belittled for our fears.

The Sacred and the Profane

This is a book about Catholic patron saints. So why are you instructed to do such things as cut a lock of hair from the head of the person you want to marry? Rub yourself with honey, rosemary, and thyme? Throw shoes over your shoulder? What do these sorts of . . . superstitious (for there's really no other appropriate word) . . . rites have to do with appealing to bona fide, Vatican-sanctioned, Roman Catholic saints to intercede with God on your behalf?

Nothing—and everything.

As we wrote this book, we discovered—amidst the familiar stories of faith, courage, grace, and compassion—a rich mosaic of folk stories and secular wisdom that, in fact, could not be separated from the legitimate religious material.

We began thinking of these folk stories as simply yet another aspect of our religious heritage. Sociologists have long pointed out that religions of all sorts share significant traits: Religions explain otherwise unexplainable aspects of life on earth; they provide moral guidelines for behavior; they create and maintain social order; and—not least—they provide a way for men and women to reconcile themselves to the inevitability of death (often by promising eternal life in some physical or spiritual form).

Formal religions have long provided men and women with reassurance—and, indeed, proof—that they have the means to control what otherwise can't be controlled. Weather, natural disasters, illness, disease, economic prosperity—these were things over which a Higher Power (or Powers) had jurisdiction and therefore could be appealed to for relief or solace in hard times.

Christianity was no different in manifesting itself through "supernatural" events (in this context, the word "supernatural" is used as meaning *not natural*, or that which goes beyond nature and science). Jesus' renown grew as a result of his miracles—supernatural acts such as raising the dead back to life, or multiplying the loaves and fishes—which were taken as proof of his close association with God.

Indeed, early Church leaders found that the most efficient way of convincing the masses that Christianity was the true faith was through publicizing the miracles performed by the apostles and other early evangelists. And what are miracles but physical proof that there *is* a God who possesses supernatural powers—and that those powers can be invoked by those on earth?

So the early "biographies" of the saints focused primarily on their miraculous powers: how they could do such supernatural things as heal sickness, foretell the future, protect against disasters or death, or control the weather. One of the earliest written records of saintly deeds, *The Golden Legend*, was enormously popular reading through the Reformation—and largely consisted of tales that recounted the saints' talent for miracle making.

Pagan rituals were especially important in medieval communities, in which agriculture was the primary economic means of survival. Chief concerns of the community revolved around the agricultural calendar (planting, growing, harvesting, preparing for winter and lean times). Other concerns were about sickness (both to humans and to all-important animals); premature death; natural disasters such as too much rain or not enough rain; and fertility and related concerns (love and marriage and the ongoing preservation of family life).

So it was a natural—and cunning—move by early Christian leaders to assimilate pagans into the new Christian faith by transforming traditional pagan rituals into Christian ones. The all-important solstice days (in summer, the longest day of the year; in winter, the shortest) and related rituals were now meant to honor Christian events and saints; other critical pagan days and forms of worship (Saman, Yule, fertility rites of spring) were likewise transformed.

Instead of traditional pagan charms, "relics" from saints—yes, that's a bit of a saint's body, or clothing, or other earthly possession—were used by newly baptized Christians to cure illness and protect against danger. Other aspects of Christianity were used in what we would now consider sacrilegious ways. Holy water was seen as holding particular magical powers. It wasn't uncommon for early Christians to drink holy water, hoping to cure a serious illness. Holy water was sprinkled on crops, on charms. Animals were baptized in the hopes that they would be protected.

As long as they didn't contain overtly pagan images, other kinds of charms were sanctioned by the Church. In the Middle Ages, the most popular Christian charm was called *Agnus dei* (Lamb of God), which was a small flat circle made of wax (originally made of special Easter candles that had been blessed by the Pope) and engraved with the image of a lamb.

This simple charm supposedly kept the devil away and protected against thunder, lightning, even death by drowning.

But there was a growing irritation among the pious regarding practices that seemed patently pagan and magical in nature. Which was one of the reasons for the religious revolution called the Reformation. Offended by the magical overtones and increasingly ritualistic aspects of the traditional Roman Catholic rites and ceremonies, the new "Protestants" banned what they considered papal nonsense, even outlawing Christmas celebrations, pointing out that most Christmas traditions were pagan in nature, related to the winter solstice and the advent of a new year. (Early Protestants even objected to marriages being celebrated in churches, under the auspices of God, as being another example of papal superstition.)

And, indeed, the Church itself took measures to emphasize the difference between so-called magic and legitimate rites used in worshiping God. In particular, it emphasized that there was a key difference between praying to the Christian God and the various kinds of secular magical and superstitious practices not sanctified by the Church.

When praying, you are asking God to do something for you—and God may or may not comply. On the other hand, those performing a magic ritual—magicians, witches, wizards, or even laypersons—are attempting to bring off the supernatural event on their own. The magic practitioner is theoretically in control—and whether his or her magic works depends on her (or his) knowledge and personal power. If done correctly, a magic ritual guarantees results.

Prayer *might* bring practical results—but is not

guaranteed to do so. You are still dependent on God deciding whether or not to take appropriate action on your behalf. And this distinction holds to this day.

In the brief biographical profiles included in the book, we have tried to take great care in distinguishing known facts from apocryphal stories, legends, or outright fictions. But if your true interest is in understanding the documented facts of the lives of the saints, there are other sources you should probably turn to. Our interest in writing this book (as will become apparent) lies in another direction.

And keep in mind: However obscure or absurd some of these stories are, the saints have long provided comfort to people on earth. What we have compiled is a collection of traditions and rituals that have been lovingly handed down from generation to generation—across geographic and socioeconomic lines.

The proper way to read (and use) this book, therefore, is less about performing the suggested rituals to exact specifications than about taking a leap of faith that, yes, spiritual help is available—if you have the courage to ask for it.

As Francis X. Weiser pointed out in his classic study of this topic, *The Handbook of Christian Feasts and Customs,* if these rituals are practiced in the right spirit, based on traditional beliefs in the existence of a benevolent host of saints in Heaven—and without what he calls "unreasonable" superstition—"this devotion to the saints' patronage provides great consolation in temporal and spiritual needs." In short, he concludes, "The fact that some patronages are based on mere legendary events does not infringe on the spiritual aspect of our petition nor on the saints' power to intercede for us."

So here is the book. Keep it by your bedside. And when you startle awake at 3:00 a.m. and your mind can't stop worrying about that difficult coworker, or that unpleasant tingling in your left leg, or the fact that your sister-in-law insists on hosting Thanksgiving dinner this year and roasting a *pig*, reach for it and see if there isn't someone who can help.

There probably is.

How a Saint Is Made:
An Illustration

Informal Phase
The candidate (who must be deceased) is "nomi-
nated" through the active (and vocal) devotion of a
group of followers. In other words, a local cult of
celebrity springs up. The fact that many official saints
were members of religious orders does not mean that
such people are inherently more holy than the general population—simply that they had more influence with the people who mattered within the
Church hierarchy. It's all who you know, isn't it?

Investigative Phase
The local bishop appoints officials to collect writings
both by the candidate and about the candidate. Witnesses give testimony about the candidate's life. Vatican checks its archives to make sure there are no black
marks on the candidate's permanent record.

Evaluation and Judgment Phase
The bishop sends this testimony and other material
to the Vatican's Congregation for the Causes of
Sainthood. Theologians and the Promoter of the
Faith judge the material. It then goes to the top—the
Pope. If he approves, then the candidate is judged
"venerable."

Miracle Process
Candidates must have a miracle ascribed to them—
and that miracle must have occurred after they have

died (miracles performed while they were living don't count). Medical experts and theologians judge the evidence.

Beatification
Once the miracle is approved by the Pope and the Cardinals, the candidate is "beatified" by the Pope.

Canonization
Before the candidate qualifies for official sainthood, another miracle is required. If all goes well, a new saint is born.

Saint Agnes

When
Love's Labors Lose

Calling on Heaven's Cupids

*The fate of love is that it always seems
too little or too much.*
——Amelia Barr

*If thou remember'st not the slightest folly
That ever love did make thee run into,
Thou hast not lov'd.*
——William Shakespeare

Having problems of the romantic sort? Take heart. A heavenly host stands by to help. The saints were once young. They were certainly human. They know what it's like to be lonely, to suffer unrequited love—or to need relief from the unwanted passion of another.

If you're in search of a soul mate, you have a wide range of choices. Or perhaps you're not quite ready for a permanent commitment—but are dying of curiosity to see who will eventually be your mate. Already in a relationship? There are saints willing to prevent your partner from philandering. There are also saints to keep stalkers at bay, help you choose between several potential lovers—or even make yourself so unattractive that no one will ever think of approaching you with romantic intentions. Well, to each his (or her) own desire. . . .

Saint Catherine of Alexandria

is one of our favorites. How could you not love someone so strong-willed, feisty, yet compassionate? Women call upon her when looking for a soul mate.

C atherine was a fourth-century pagan Egyptian princess (daughter of the emperor Costus), beautiful, intelligent—and outspoken. She succeeded to the throne at age fourteen, and her subjects urged her to marry. But she was particular. First, she refused the hand of the Roman emperor Maxentius because she did not love him. Then, she let it be known that her groom must possess four essential traits: He must be so nobly born that all would worship him; so great that he would not be indebted to her for being made king; so beautiful that angels should desire to look upon him; and so benevolent as to forgive all who offended him.

This narrowed her choice considerably. Legend says the Virgin Mary appeared to a local hermit, suggesting Jesus Christ as Catherine's suitor. Catherine considered it, but then dreamed that Christ rejected her, saying, "She's not fair enough." Catherine understood this as a sign, and converted to Christianity. That very night Mary visited Catherine in a dream, along with Jesus, who this time was favorably disposed toward Catherine. In the vision, they were married. When Catherine awoke, she wore a wedding ring, but one that only she could see.

Maxentius, still hot on her trail, tried to humble Catherine by pitting her against fifty pagan philosophers in a grand faith-debate extravaganza. She won what was for her the ultimate prize: She converted every one of them. Maxentius killed all the newly converted philosophers but still had hopes for a tryst with Catherine. When she rejected him once more, she was beaten and tied to a wheel. (This is the origin of the "Catherine wheel" later found in the dungeons of the more sophisticated religious torturers.) Not only did angels miraculously appear and destroy the wheel, but Catherine managed to convert the two hundred soldiers who were guarding her.

Maxentius responded to her industriousness by beheading every one of the soldiers. He also lopped off Catherine's head. But instead of blood, milk—the symbol of fertility, nutrition, and healing—flowed from her head and torso. She was carried by angels to Mount Sinai, where Saint Catherine's Monastery is now located. After her death, the mark of a wedding ring is said to have appeared on her finger.

Catherine posthumously was made a Doctor of the Catholic Church because of her knowledge. Since she was also a mystical bride of Christ, she is the patron saint for women seeking mates. Her steadfast—and ultimately fatal—devotion to her faith made her the prototype for a special category of saints, "the virgin martyrs," each of whom rejected some man's hand because of personal or religious scruples, and paid dearly for it.

Here's What You Can Say:

A husband, Saint Catherine,
A good one, Saint Catherine,
A handsome one, Saint Catherine,
A rich one, Saint Catherine,
And soon, Saint Catherine!

And Here's What You Can Do:

You need to get your hands on a lock of the hair of the person you want to marry. Okay, so it's the middle of the night and he's in Boise, you're in Delaware. Go ahead, sketch it. An approximation will do fine. Put the lock under your pillow while saying one of the prayers included here. Sleep on it for three nights straight. Lighting a candle is also recommended before you say your prayer—but don't forget to blow it out before you fall asleep. According to folklore, if Catherine grants your request, you will be married to the owner of the hair by the next Saint Catherine's Day (November 25). Supplicant, beware! Obtain the lock of hair by means that won't get you arrested.

Bonus Ritual!

(This prayer can be used interchangeably with the preceding.)

Sweet Saint Catherine,

send me a husband,

A good one, I pray,

But anyone better than none.

O Saint Catherine, lend me thine aid,

That I may not die an old maid.

Odd Saint Fact:

Saint Catherine's Monastery has survived unmolested despite the political and religious turmoil of the surrounding region—which is currently Israel—by a reported direct command of the prophet Mohammed.

Saint Catherine of Alexandria (Feast Day: November 25) is also patroness of lawyers, librarians, nurses, and schoolgirls. She can be invoked against diseases of the tongue.

We're also quite fond of Saint Agnes.
As the patron of virgins, she is useful if you'd
like a glimpse of your future mate (even if you're
perfectly happy sowing your wild oats for the
present, but just need some reassurance that eventually someone will be sharing your pillow).

Agnes has long been an ally of the unmarried,
probably because of the difficulties she had
while single. Despite her young age—just thirteen
when she died in the year 304—Agnes is famous for
the relentless passion of her many suitors. The most
ardent and well known was Eutropius, the Roman
governor's son. Agnes told Eutropius that she was
already taken, and by a much more worthy and powerful suitor (meaning God). Since Eutropius could
not hope to compete with Agnes's sacred intended, he
went to his daddy, who summoned the young girl to
appear before him.

Eutropius's father first offered Agnes troves of riches
and other social privileges for taking his loutish son
off his hands, but she refused. Then Eutropius senior
threatened to torture her. Still Agnes remained firm,

even after being treated to a guided tour of the family torture chambers. Finally, he brought out the really big guns. Agnes was stripped naked and led publicly through the streets. Her final destination was to be the local brothel. Yet even that attempt to shame her into submission failed; Agnes's hair grew as she walked, protecting her modesty and dignity, and at the brothel an angel appeared and clothed her in a shining white garment.

The white garment proved too much for Eutropius senior. He gave up entreating on behalf of his son and instead tried to force himself on young Agnes. He was struck blind on the spot. Naturally, our Agnes took pity on him and gave him back his eyesight.

That good deed was most certainly not left unpunished. Agnes was subsequently accused of witchcraft and executed. She went to her death not only willingly, but joyfully.

Here's What You Can Say:

Sweet Saint Agnes, work thee fast

If ever I be to marry man,

Or ever man to marry me,

I hope him this night to see.

And Here's What You Can Do:

For women: So you want to know who you're going to marry? Go to the kitchen. Do not say a word. Do not turn on the radio or television. Do not eat anything. Mix together an egg, a cup of water, a half cup of flour, and a dash of salt. (Yes, it will look disgusting.) Carve your initials on the cake, and bake it for twenty minutes at 350 degrees. When it's done, take it out of the oven and recite the preceding prayer. That night you will dream of your future husband. Don't eat the cake! (You wouldn't enjoy it anyway.)

If this seems like too much work, here's another method. Fast for twenty-four hours. That's right—don't eat anything for a full day and night. Then, right before bed, eat a boiled egg with salt on it. Say the preceding prayer. You will dream of your future husband. Don't worry if he's surrounded by pizzas and cream puffs. That's just your hunger talking.

Men wanting to see their wife-to-be must eat a raw herring—yes, the whole thing, including bones—before going to bed. Keep the bicarbonate of soda handy.

Bonus Ritual!

Go someplace you've never been before (and be prepared to spend the night). Before going to sleep, take your right sock and tie the left one around it while saying the following:

I knit this now.

This knot I knit.

To know the thing I know not yet.

That I may see the man

that shall my husband be.

Not in his best array,

But what he weareth every day.

That tomorrow I may him ken,

From among all other men.*

*If seeking a female romantic partner, change the prayer accordingly.

Then lie down with your hands under your head. Your future spouse will appear in a dream and seal the knot with a kiss. Extra credit if you fast for twenty-four hours before performing this rite. (Traditionally, this, like many other rituals, was used on the eve of the saint's feast day. But try it, even out of season. Agnes is likely to take pity on you.)

Bonus Ritual (II)!

When the course of your love is not running smoothly:

Take one sprig of rosemary, another of thyme. Sprinkle them three times each with water. Place one sprig in each of your shoes. Place one shoe on either side of your bed. Say the following:

Saint Agnes,

Who is to lovers kind,

Come ease the trouble of my mind.

Saint Agnes (Feast Day: January 21) is also the patron saint of Girl Scouts.

Saint Wilgefortis (also known as Saint Uncumber, Saint Livrade, and Saint Liberata) is an extremely useful ally in discouraging unwanted would-be romantic partners. "No" should mean "no." But when it doesn't, there's always this bearded lady to intercede on your behalf.

Wilgefortis was one of a litter of septuplets—all girls—born to the king of Portugal. Although each of Wilgefortis's unfortunate sisters was also martyred, each to the Christian cause, hers is the story that remains active in our collective imagination.

Wilgefortis's father, a pagan, wanted her to marry the neighboring king of Sicily. However, Wilgefortis had other plans, having already on her own initiative converted to Christianity and vowed to—what else?—remain celibate. So far, so good. But here's where the Wilgefortis story veers from the norm of other beautiful-and-devout-but-doomed virgins. Rather than endure the physical tortures of a Catherine, or an Agnes, who had her breasts cut off, Wilgefortis hit upon the brilliant idea of making herself sexually undesirable. She prayed to be made so unattractive that no man would want her. Her reward? She promptly grew an impressive mustache and beard.

Wilgefortis first became a significant cult figure in fourteenth-century Flanders, when women began praying for her help in unburdening themselves of unwanted husbands. A tradition grew of building a shrine to Wilgefortis, offering oats for her blessing, and then feeding the blessed oats to the horse of the unwanted husband. Why be so kind to the horse? In the hopes it would swiftly take the undesirable husband away.

Like Saint Christopher, Wilgefortis is officially deemed legend, not saint. And the origins of her story are a bit murky, although the first confirmed telling of it comes from Gregory the Great. But many scholars believe it originates in the town of Lucca, Italy, where a famous crucifix has long been displayed in the local church. The long gown and bejeweled head of the Christ figure on this crucifix (which is fairly typical of the religious art of the period) makes it appear female, despite the obvious presence of a beard and mustache on its face. The questionable sex of this particular venerated image, scholars now conjecture, is what led to the Wilgefortis story of the stubbornly pious bearded lady.

The reason for all the forms of her name (she is called Uncumber in England, Livrade in France, and Liberata in southern Europe) is due to the soft spot Wilgefortis had for the plight of unhappy wives. Not surprisingly, many prominent (and mostly male) members of the church found fault with the ritual of offering oats on an altar in the hopes that a horse would "uncumber" a woman of an unsuitable husband. Sir Thomas More decried the practice as "despicable." Still, the cult endures to this day throughout Europe. And we see no reason to limit her generous help to women only; men, too, should feel free to use her whenever they feel romantically crowded by an overzealous admirer.

Here's What You Can Do:

Light a candle and surround it with oats (Cheerios will do).

And Here's What You Can Say:

Saint Wilgefortis, please
take away this bothersome suitor
(name him or her),
uncumber me

from his/her unwanted affections,

and liberate me

from any responsibility to respond

to his/her entreaties.

Odd Saint Fact:

The crucifix that is believed to have inspired the Wilgefortis legend had to have its feet replaced—because the multitude of pilgrims who came to pray there wore away the original wooden feet. In order to prevent the same thing from recurring, the new feet were made of silver.

Saint Wilgefortis's Feast Day is July 20.

$Saint$ $Luke$ (the $Evangelist$) is commonly called upon throughout $Europe$ by women who wish to evoke a vision of their future mate. As always, men should be welcome to avail themselves of this saintly help.

Luke was a Greek physician and an early evangelist for Christianity. A disciple of the apostle Paul, Luke accompanied Paul on many of his missionary journeys. He wrote about them in his version of the gospel, which is considered the most eloquent, humanitarian, and sympathetic toward the poor and toward women. It was Luke who gave us many of the most beloved parables, including those of the Good Samaritan, the Prodigal Son, and the Good Thief.

No one is sure why Luke has become associated with courtship rituals. One possible reason is that he is so obviously sympathetic to women; he especially revered Mary, the mother of Christ, and devoted many passages of his gospel to details of her life. Luke gave us the most dramatically realized version of Mary's visit to her cousin Elizabeth, as well as the phrase "Hail Mary, full of grace," which became part of the Hail Mary prayer.

In a more secular vein, since Saint Luke's feast day, October 18, occurs around the traditional time of harvest, many pagan ceremonies related to the agricultural calendar—and most revolving around all sorts of primitive pleasures, including "courtship"— have become attached to Luke. A bawdy "Horn Faire" was formerly held in Kent, England, in which all sorts of misbehavior was excused under the guise of paying tribute to Saint Luke (men dressed up as women and played tricks on townsfolk, and everyone drank liberally). One possible explanation for this particular Luke-ian celebration is that since Saint Luke's traditional emblem was an ox, the "horns" of the beast were somehow mistakenly taken as the symbol for cuckoldry, leading to this dubious festival.

Here's What You Can Do:

Those wishing to have a vision of their future mate should mix together the herbs marjoram, marigold, thyme, and wormwood along with honey and vinegar. Anoint yourself (be warned: you will be very sticky).

Saint Luke, Saint Luke,
Be kind to me
In dreams let me my true love see.

Odd Saint Fact:

The phrase "lukewarm" comes from the fact that Saint Luke's feast day in mid-autumn is often blessed with very pleasant weather—neither too hot, nor too cold, but *luke*warm. Get it?

Saint Luke's Feast Day is October 18, and he is also the patron saint of artists and surgeons.

And, of course, there's Saint Valentine, one of the few saints to make it onto our modern secular calendar. Indeed, he hardly requires introduction as the patron saint of lovers. He can be used to help you choose your one true love. It's a shame his feast day has also been responsible for more lovelorn worrying than any other day of the year.

Valentine is actually one of the least plausible of the saints. There are many who question whether he existed at all; others believe he is a composite of several early Christian martyrs renowned for their chastity. The most likely candidates included an early Persian Christian convert stoned to death in Rome, and a bishop martyred at Terni. Not much more is known of either man. Yet everyone associates Valentine with romantic love.

The association of Valentine with romantic rites is due to the largely futile efforts of early religious Christian leaders to do away with pagan festivals by substituting a Christian observance. February 14 was traditionally the Roman festival of Lupercalia, an important day to honor Juno, the Queen of Heaven and protector of women. The wife of Jupiter, Juno was said to bestow her blessing on courtship rituals or marriages celebrated that day. She was also believed to give girls good luck when playing romantic games of chance (sweethearts were often drawn by lottery). All these superstitions and rituals were transferred to Saint Valentine as Christianity spread. Another pagan connection between Valentine and romance is that birds were believed to choose their mates for the season in mid-February, close to the feast of Saint Valentine.

Here's What You Can Do:

$\mathcal{P}$ut slips of paper containing the names of potential lovers into a bowl (or cup, or hat). Reach into the container and choose one of the slips of paper.

And Here's What You Can Say:

Thou art my love and I am thine
I draw . . . for my Valentine.

Whichever name you choose will be yours by the next Valentine's Day (February 14).

For women, the first bird seen on Saint Valentine's day will indicate the sort of man her husband will be. A blackbird indicates a clergyman; a goldfinch (or any yellow bird), a rich man; a crossbill means an argumentative, mean man; and doves and bluebirds are good and happy men respectively.

Beware—if you see or hear a woodpecker on Saint Valentine's Day, you will never marry.

Saint Valentine's Feast Day is February 14. When in doubt, send roses.

For true love, skip the Personals and take a cue from the Mexican tradition: Invoke Saint Martin de Porres, a Peruvian saint-of-all-trades.

Born in 1579, Saint Martin was the son of a Spanish nobleman/soldier; his mother was a freed African slave who had made Peru her home. At that time, a handful of Spaniards (approximately 2,000 total) was attempting to rule the indigenous population of 25,000 native Indians, as well as the 40,000 Africans who had been imported as slaves. The various inhabitants of Peru were in agreement only in their distrust of each other—and in their aversion to any child born of mixed race. Martin's own parents never married, and his father even refused to officially acknowledge his paternity of this dark-skinned son. He did, however, make sure Martin would be able to make a living, by apprenticing him to a barber. In those days, a barber was also turned to for medical advice—and as it turned out, Martin had a knack for healing. He became locally renowned for his ability to cure the sick. (Martin is also patron saint of hairdressers, in case you're interested.)

Eventually walking away from his barber chair, Martin used his medical powers in the poorer communities and among the slave population in Peru. Martin spurned any attempt to cash in on his hairstyling or medical talents, but instead handed all earnings over to the poor. Eventually deciding to devote his life to God, Martin entered the local Dominican monastery as a tertiary (the lowest notch on the totem pole of organized religious life). Frequently taunted for both his skin color and his lowly status, Martin would only shrug good-naturedly and redouble his efforts to do good work for the community.

One of the first recorded "holistic" healers, Martin believed in treating the whole person, not just the specific injury or illness. He listened to his patients, personally bathed them and changed their clothes, and gave them spiritual advice.

Over the years, as the Martin legend grew, it was whispered that he was often seen working miracles in more than one place simultaneously. Folklore says even wounded and sick animals sought him out. And it appears that Martin was a Dr. Dolittle of sorts—able to talk to animals, even scheduling appointments that they promptly kept. (There's an interesting image:

"Mr. Cat, I will see you at three p.m. on Thursday, after your fifth nap.") His broad compassion has lent his life to many interesting patronages: In Mexico, he's invoked for true love; in Guatemala, to protect beloved animals; and worldwide he is invoked on behalf of racial and social justice.

Here's What You Can Do:

Turn a picture or statue of Saint Martin on his head. (This bit about punishing obviously eager-to-please saints always puzzles us.) Place a glass of water in front of him. Say the following prayer. When your request for true love has been granted, you can turn Saint Martin right side up again.

And Here's What You Can Say:

Dear Saint Martin,

Be with me

In my struggles to find a soul mate

And in my desire to love all people

without exception

And without regard for race, color,

or creed

As God does.

Saint Martin de Porres's Feast Day is November 3.

Saint Monica is your best counselor when you're seeking help with your marriage.

Monica, mother of Saint Augustine, struggled with addiction, marital woes, and unruly children nearly her whole life. It's no wonder that she is invoked for help in stressful family situations.

Reportedly a heavy drinker, Monica was forced into an arranged marriage with a pagan—and an angry, hard-drinking, verbally abusive one at that. Her children ran wild. And—just when things couldn't get any worse—her mother-in-law moved in.

Monica first conquered her own drinking problem. Next she managed to dry out her alcoholic husband (and convince him not to stray to brothels and other women), then converted both him and his odious mother, all the while raising three decidedly unruly children: Augustine (eventually to be the famous Saint Augustine), Perpetua, and Navigius. Augustine gave her the most, and the most famous, trouble. To be honest, Monica sounds a bit batty; she followed Augustine everywhere and implored her friends to pray on Augustine's behalf. Even the parish priest apparently ran for cover when he saw her coming. Eventually, Monica was convinced to take a less physically active role in Augustine's conversion, and devoted her time and energy to fasting, praying, and holding vigils. It took seventeen long years, but Augustine finally converted. Monica died that same year—happy, we imagine—since she declared upon her deathbed that "all my hopes in this world are now fulfilled."

Here's What You Can Do:

Place a flower or plant in an empty wine bottle. Around the bottle place those things that conjure up pleasant memories of your marriage: photos, your wedding ring, or a souvenir from a happy trip.

And Here's What You Can Say:

Dear Saint Monica,
Give me the strength
To pull myself and my family
together.
Help me see the way
To move ahead
with dignity and hope.

Saint Monica's Feast Day is August 27.

Saint Thérèse of Lisieux

Coping with Anxiety

Let the True Experts Help You
Achieve Spiritual Tranquillity

*You must learn to be still
in the midst of activity
and to be vibrantly alive in repose.*
—Indira Gandhi

*The most spiritual human beings,
assuming they are the most courageous,
also experience by far the most painful
tragedies; but it is precisely
for this reason that they honor life,
because it brings against them its most
formidable weapons.*
—Friedrich Nietzsche

All of us experience times of extreme anxiety and stress. Does it seem to be getting worse, not better? We think so, as the already frantic pace of life continues to accelerate. Take heart. You've got the best of the best standing by to give you help—both by example (how they lived their lives)—and by intercession.

Saint Mary Magdalen, not surprisingly, is the patron of repentant sinners, those who truly regret their past errors and who are sincere in their wish to do better.

There are a number of stories in the Bible about so-called fallen women (usually, that meant a prostitute) who were treated compassionately by Jesus despite the scorn heaped upon him—even by his own apostles—for bothering with such lowly sinners. One such beautiful, proud, but not notoriously sinful, woman sought Jesus out when he was having dinner at a rich man's house. She fell at Jesus' feet, kissing them and wetting them with her tears before drying them with her hair. (Jesus told her, "Thy faith has saved thee. Go in peace.") Luke told of another woman who had seven devils cast out of her with Jesus' help. Scholars differ on whether or not these were the same as the Mary Magdalene, sister of Martha and Lazarus, who stood with the Virgin Mary by his cross as Jesus was crucified, and to whom the risen Christ appeared on Easter morning. (We do know that this Mary was called "Magdalen" because she had long lived in the town of Magdale, near Galilee.) Whatever the facts, Mary Magdalene has come to be associated with sinners who have truly repented.

The Mary Magdalene who was the sister of Martha and Lazarus was reputed to have had a long and productive life in service of spreading Christ's word. A stellar character after she reformed, one legend says she traveled, with the Blessed Virgin and John the Apostle to Ephesus and was responsible for converting that region. Another has her engaged briefly to John the Apostle; another, that she moved to France and lived as a hermit. (Her supposed home as a hermit, La Sainte Baume, or "The Holy Cave," near Marseilles, is the primary shrine to Mary Magdalene—and was *the* hot destination spot in the Middle Ages; nearly every French king in recorded history has visited, and to this day thousands of pilgrims still make the trek.)

Whatever her story, Mary Magdalene has a strong cult to this day, as she is seen as utterly human and a model for the comforting philosophy that it is never too late to change—or be forgiven. She is frequently used as an example of the true compassion of Christ, that he did not reject her because of her past sins, but looked into her heart and saw true repentance.

Here's What You Can Do:

Bake a loaf of unadorned bread—muffins will do, as long as they're nutritious. Give them to friends or loved ones (or strangers)—anyone who looks hungry.

And Here's What You Can Say:

Dearest Mary Magdalene,

Help me change my ways

See how I acknowledge my faults

And witness my determination

to do better.

Mary Magdalene's Feast Day is July 22.

Blessed Julian of Norwich

can be called upon for relief in times of extreme stress no matter what the cause.

Born in 1342, Julian is best known for her work *Revelations of Divine Love,* which reveals sixteen different mystical visions of Jesus. Her most controversial insight, now considered particularly interesting to feminist religious scholars, portrays Jesus as the mother of Christianity (not that Jesus was female but that the role he played was a creative, nurturing, maternal one).

Julian is also renowned for her vision of Jesus placing the entire universe in her hand, in the form of a hazelnut. "What may this be?" she marveled. Jesus replied, "It is all that is made."

Scholars are unsure when she received her "revelations," or visions of Christ, that were recorded in her

Revelations. Indeed, very little is known about the personal life of Julian, although her *Revelations* is generally seen as a "spiritual diary." Since her writing focused on finding God in the depths of one's self, it bears a strong resemblance to writings of other contemplative faiths such as Buddhism, Hinduism, and Jewish mysticism. Her imaginative approach—she wasn't big on dogma—influenced twentieth-century writers such as T. S. Eliot and Iris Murdoch. Although Julian was never canonized as a saint, her *Revelations* continues to be relevant to religious scholars and general readers alike.

Here's What You Can Say:

All shall be well,
And all shall be well,
And all manner of thing
shall be well.

And Here's What You Can Do:

Find a grove of trees, take a leaf from the ground, or a twig if in winter. With the twig or leaf in hand walk among the trees repeating the above prayer.

Odd Saint Fact:

Julian was known as an "anchoress," which meant she shut herself off from the world to pray in solitude. Anchoresses were thought to bring spiritual benefits to a town, and so all fashionable towns wanted at least one. An anchoress is made in a peculiar ceremony. With the local bishop reciting the Mass for the Dead, the candidate dons her religious habit and walks into the cell—the small, barren room in which the anchoress will live—as if into a grave, the attending bishop sprinkling ashes in her wake.

Blessed Julian of Norwich's Feast Day is May 8.

Saint Thérèse of Lisieux can be invoked to ease an overcomplicated or stress-filled life. Her mode of existence —it's not easy to follow—is to simplify, simplify.

This petite nineteenth-century Frenchwoman did not, at first glance, accomplish anything extraordinary. No impassioned or frustrated suitors. No bloody tortures on account of her faith. She lived quietly and simply as a Carmelite nun, never achieved any position of power or authority, and died when she was just twenty-four. Yet Thérèse has slowly achieved a reputation as one of the most powerful patron saints you can summon for help in times of emotional turmoil. She was called the "Little Flower" on account of her quiet manner and delicate physical presence, and multiple miracles and healings have been attributed to her.

Thérèse was born in 1873 in Alençon, the daughter of a mother who yearned to be a saint and a father who had hoped to become a monk. But they fell in love and decided to marry. How to combine their spiritual aspirations with their earthly ones? With their wedding vows they also took a vow of celibacy. However, human nature being what it is, they ended up having nine children.

Only five of these children survived—all girls—and they each seemed to have caught their parents' religious fervor. After the mother died (very young), their father, now earning his living as a watchmaker, moved them to Lisieux, where he had a sister who could help him raise his pious brood. One by one, each of the girls entered the nearby Carmelite convent.

Thérèse, the youngest, had been only four when her mother died. Always a slight and emotional girl, Thérèse was cured of a serious illness when still very young after having a vision of the Virgin Mary. By age eleven, she was slipping out of her bed and prostrating herself in front of her bedroom wall to engage in hours of contemplative prayer. Her emotions, never steady to begin with, began to careen wildly. She refused to do any housework, and cried at the slightest provocation. She prayed for stoicism, and was rewarded at age fourteen by what she would later term her "conversion," which manifested itself in her ability to master her own violent emotions and to place the concerns of others before her own. By age fifteen, she was ready to take her vows but was initially denied because of her youth. Her father accompanied her on a pilgrimage to Rome with the goal of petitioning the Pope himself. According to legend, Thérèse made such a fuss when she was forbidden entrance to the Vatican that she had to be forcefully restrained and carried out by two burly guards. Still, she ultimately made her point and became a nun.

Thérèse frequently fell asleep during prayers and never advanced past novice, although she is recorded as otherwise having followed the rigorous and austere Carmelite life with great respect and obedience. Her health began deteriorating very early (she eventually died of tuberculosis), but after praying for guidance, she made peace with the fact that she would never perform the heroic deeds she'd dreamed of. "It is impossible for me to grow bigger, so I put up with myself as I am, with all my countless faults," she said.

Her intense spiritual ambition—she wanted to be a priest, or a martyr—allowed her to view her approaching death as a blessing. Indeed, she saw it as symbolic, as it came at the exact age at which she would have been ordained if male. She finally grew to accept what her vocation must have been, since she was not suited for the rigors of an active life. "It is love," she said. She vowed to return and perform many miracles. "I will spend my heaven doing good on earth," she promised. Fans of Thérèse have invoked her help for everything from seeking true love to finding the right job. However, her life has also always been an inspiration for those seeking a peaceful existence.

In her short but celebrated autobiography, *The Story of a Soul,* Thérèse advocated a life of quiet obedience and devotion, stressing the joy to be found in performing single daily chores rather than striving for feats of great strength or courage. We think of Thérèse when we recall Mother Teresa's famous words about her own life of steady adherence to what might be considered thankless labor: "We can do no great things, only little things with love."

Little Flower,
In this hour
Show your power.

$\mathcal{F}$ind a quiet place. Light a candle (a red or pink one is best—a rose-scented one is perfect) next to a picture of Saint Thérèse. Place roses (real, fake, or even drawn) at the picture, and repeat a prayer that includes Thérèse's famous words—those she uttered on her deathbed as a vow that she would continue her good work from heaven—"I will let fall a shower of roses."

Dear Saint Thérèse,
Let a shower of roses fall
Let a shower of roses fall
Let a shower of roses fall
I need your help.

$\mathcal{I}$f you want, you can try this more traditional Catholic prayer to the Little Flower:

Saint Thérèse, the Little Flower,
Please pick me a rose
from the heavenly garden

Send it to me
With a message of love
Ask God to grant me
the favor I implore
And tell him I will love him
each day more and more.

Say the above prayer for five straight days, each time followed by five Hail Marys, five Our Fathers, and five Glory Be's.

Odd Saint Fact:

One of the more charming aspects of the Thérèse legend says that when she agrees to intercede on your behalf, she will send you a flower as acknowledgment. Many people claim to have smelled roses after requesting Saint Thérèse's aid.

Saint Thérèse of Lisieux's Feast Day is October 1.

For calm and courage in the face of adversity, you can always entreat help from Saint Joan of Arc, the intrepid Maid of Orléans.

Joan needs little introduction, so well-known is her story. At the age of fourteen, this simple farmer's daughter had a vision—a blaze of light in which the voices of Catherine and Margaret, two powerful early female saints, instructed her to leave her father's farm and help France defend itself against English invaders. Joan obeyed. In the face of nearly unimaginable scorn and disbelief from anyone she told of these voices (which continued ceaselessly giving her instructions throughout her military career), Joan managed to work her way through the bureaucracy of the army and carry her point all the way to the claimant to the French throne, the dauphin, later Charles VII. Somehow, she persuaded Charles to let her lead a band of soldiers to Orléans. This young spitfire wore white armor and carried her own special banner. Although seriously wounded by an arrow shot directly into her chest, she nevertheless led her guys to victory, and lived to have a place of honor at the side of Charles when he was finally crowned king at Rheims in 1429.

Naturally, it was all downhill from Charles VII's crowning. Joan knew from her friendly voices that she was living on borrowed time. Suspicion and jealousy of her grew from all sides: the court, the Church, the army. Even Charles abandoned her at the end, show-ing—at least for the saintly inclined—that no good deed goes unpunished. The Duke of Burgundy cap-tured and imprisoned her, and sold her to the English. Never overly fond of our girl Joan (who, after all, had been responsible for their defeat), the Brits put her on trial for witchcraft, during which the simple unschooled farm girl was taunted and ultimately con-demned for her lack of formal theological knowledge. In a move that was guaranteed to get her a major mo-tion picture deal, Joan was burned at the stake in 1431. She showed her great and good courage to the fiery end.

Joan can be invoked for courage in the face of what-ever emotional or physical battle you are fighting: whether against pain, grief, or fear itself. She's espe-cially good for people who somehow manage to flout convention as they seek their own path through life.

Saint Joan,
Lend me your strength
Be present
As I face this current danger
Let your courage be mine.

And Here's What You Can Do:

Write Joan's name on a white ribbon, along with the word "Courage." Tie the ribbon around your wrist when you feel in need of help.

Odd Saint Fact:

Entirely unofficially, Joan is raucously celebrated each year at Chicago's Gay Pride Parade as the patron saint of cross-dressers.

Saint Joan of Arc's Feast Day is May 30. Joan is also patron of soldiers and of France.

When you're feeling blue, ask Saint John the Baptist for his aid. No, you might not want to throw away your Prozac. But even though God does tend to help those who help themselves, it certainly doesn't hurt to have Saint John on your side too.

Saint John the Baptist has always been a Big Saint throughout the Christian world. He had the talent, the personality, and the family connections. (Elizabeth, John's mother, was Mary's cousin, making John a second cousin to Jesus.)

Elizabeth was past the age of childbearing when an angel visited her and her husband, Zacharias, foretelling the birth of a son who would be a prophet. John duly arrived, and devoted his life to preparing everyone for the coming of the Messiah. Although little is known of his early life, he suffered hardship and solitude while preparing himself spiritually for Jesus' arrival. He wandered alone through the deserts of Judea, fasting and praying, wearing only animal skins, eating wild honey and locusts, and preaching repentance to anyone he stumbled across. Eventually he set up a permanent camp of sorts by the River Jordan and offered anyone who was interested a chance to be baptized. When Jesus arrived one day and asked to be baptized, John saw the Holy Spirit descend upon him, and immediately proclaimed him the true Messiah.

John never took the easy way in life. He publicly denounced Herod Antipas, governor of Galilee, for marrying his half brother's wife, Herodias. Herod didn't appreciate the commentary, and John ended up in prison. You know the rest: Herodias's daughter, Salome, danced for Herod at his birthday feast, enticing him into promising her anything she wanted. At the urging of her mother, Salome asked for John's head on a platter. That was the end of John's life on earth, but just the beginning of his influence on the theology and practices of the Church.

If any of the John the Baptist–related advice sounds closer to magic than to traditional Catholic theology, that's because these rituals and superstitions are largely pagan in origin. Saint John's feast day happens to fall around the summer solstice, or Midsummer's Day, which figures prominently throughout the world as a time of magic and mystery. People have long celebrated the light (summer) and prepared for the darkness and cold (the coming winter) on this day. On Midsummer Night's Eve the traditional bonfires lit on hilltops throughout Europe are thought to protect against evil and illness in the coming year; the wild dancing around these bonfires is meant to ensure fertility (for people, crops, and animals) as well as general good luck. There are too many folk rituals that have come to be associated with Saint John to list here, and some of them are truly weird, if not gruesome (there are ways to predict who will die in the coming year, as well as spells to become invisible). We prefer to think of all these in symbolic terms: It was Saint John's mission to prepare us for the coming of Christ and to repel the darkness of spiritual ignorance, and we take all this "white magic" associated with him in the same generous spirit.

Here's What You Can Do:

If you are feeling depressed or anxious:

Light a fire, and throw into it pieces of paper on which you have written your worries and anxieties or hopes for the coming year. If you don't have a fireplace, or a place outside where you can safely build a fire, a candle will do.

Hang some St. John's wort in your doorway to repel the bad spirits (including your own low spirits).

$\mathcal{J}$f you are trying to conceive:

Take some St. John's wort while walking naked in your garden after midnight. Do not speak. Folklore says you will be pregnant within the year. Supplicant beware: Always check with your doctor before taking St. John's wort.

$\mathcal{T}$o bring back an ex-love:

Take three roses. Bury one under an evergreen tree or bush, another in a shallow hole in the ground. Place the third under your pillow. Leave the rose under your pillow for three nights, then burn it. Tradition says that your ex-love will be troubled night and day by thoughts of you until he or she returns. Make sure not to tell anyone you are doing this, or it will not work.

St. John's wort, before its popularity as a natural antidepressant, was used by voodoo conjurers and folk medicine practitioners to ward off evil spirits. The leaves and petals contain oil, and the pigment-filled glands appear as reddish spots in sunlight. According to legend, these spots are Saint John's blood, and the plant is most potent if rituals are performed on his birthday, which is also his feast day.

Saint John the Baptist's Feast Day is June 24.

Attempting to break a bad habit or two? Need help resisting temptations of the world? Try a dose of Saint Augustine.

Any saint who said, "Give me chastity and continence, but not yet," as Augustine did, is bound to have fans. Later in his life, of course, Augustine was as passionately devout and pure of mind and spirit as any virgin martyr could hope to be. His writings—particularly his *Confessions*—are read for their beauty and literary merit as well as spiritual wisdom.

This reassuringly human saint was born in Algeria of a pagan father and a devoutly Christian mother, Saint Monica (see page 40). At first he was determined to be a lawyer, but he gave that up for a life of wine and women, living so dissolutely that he fathered a son out of wedlock. Although it took more than seventeen years of fast living, through the persistent prayers of his mother Augustine finally converted. He found himself so full of bitterness at the thought of his wasted youth that he threw himself into the dust in a garden, crying, "How long more, O Lord? Why does not this hour put an end to my sins?" Soon afterward he found and took to heart Saint Paul's advice to "put away all impurities." His writings remain some of the most influential in history, and include such jewels of wisdom as "Habit, if not resisted, soon becomes necessity." He saw the bright side to temperance: "Where your pleasure is, there your treasure / Where your treasure, there your heart / Where your heart, there your happiness."

Here's What You Can Say:

When asking God for help with a bad habit:

Give me whatever you ask of me
Then ask of me what you will
Remember that we are only dust
For of the dust you made us.

And Here's What You Can Do:

Take a symbol of your habit (cigarette, wine label, candy wrapper) and bury it in a garden. Extra credit if you plant flowers near it. Say the above prayer.

Saint Augustine's Feast Day is August 28.

Sleepless in Seattle, Syracuse, or San Francisco? Call on The Seven Sleepers of Ephesus before you reach for those sleeping pills. . . .

Saint Gregory of Tours first wrote down the story of the Seven Sleepers, but most historians believe that the legend hails from before the sixth century. Scholars often cite these slumbering seven as the Christian version of other "oversleeping" fables, such as Rip Van Winkle.

Here's how Saint Gregory's version goes: Seven young Christian men refused to pay tribute to the pagan gods, and instead fled to a cave on Mount Celion. When the emperor Decius discovered their whereabouts, he ordered the cave blocked with stones so that the young men would die of starvation. The seven were deemed to be martyrs, and their grave was marked as such by later Christians. However the story goes, they were not dead—God had merely put them to sleep, and they slumbered happily for two hundred years, long after the demise of Decius. When they awoke, they found Ephesus now embraced Christianity. After long and apparently happy lives, they died of natural causes and were buried in the same cave they had slept in for two centuries.

Here's What You Can Do:

Take a slow breath. After exhaling, say the following prayer. Repeat seven times.

And Here's What You Can Say:

I pray for rest that is sorely needed.

You, Blessed Sleepers of Ephesus,

can watch this night

and bring to me the security

I need to close my eyes,

with the knowledge that no harm

will come to me

or my loved ones while I slumber.

The Seven Sleepers of Ephesus's Feast Day is July 27.

Need a recipe for a good sleep? You could try a warm cup of milk, or a quick appeal to Saint John of the Cross.

John was a mystic, that is, he had visions that allowed him to form an intimate spiritual relationship with God. Many of his religious poems read like love poems. He sounds positively smitten in such works as his *Spiritual Canticle,* in which he entreats God, "Why have you hidden away, lover? / and left me grieving / care on care?" The beauty of his poetry and the profundity of his visions have made him greatly beloved as a writer as well as a saint.

But John had a rough time of it. His father, Gonzalo de Yepes, was a minor Spanish nobleman who ventured out of his social milieu and married a poor orphan, Catalina Alvarez, only to die in 1544, two years after his third son, Juan de Yepes, or John, was born. Gonzalo had been ostracized from his family because of his marriage—in addition to coming from a lower class, his wife was of Moorish descent. This was sure to draw attention, which is the last thing the de Yepes family wanted, since they were *convertos*, or Jews who converted to Christianity to escape the Spanish Inquisition. Persecution was rampant; anyone with Jewish—or Moorish—roots was always in danger of being exiled, or worse. Gonzalo's widow and children had no recourse but to travel from town to town in search of sustenance. John was eventually placed in a boarding school for poor children, where he received a Christian education. He joined the Carmelite order and was ordained a priest in 1567.

On his return to the city of Medina del Campo, where his mother and brothers had settled and were making a living of sorts as weavers, John hooked up with Teresa of Avila, who became his mystical mentor. Both John and Teresa worked diligently to reform what they saw as lax practices within the Carmelite communities (both male and female), and John was at one point thrown into jail. It was while in prison that he wrote his famous poem, *The Dark Night of the Soul*. Again, he rhapsodized longingly that "upon my flowering breast, which I kept wholly for him alone, there he lay sleeping, and I caressing him there in a breeze from the fanning cedars." John used his physical suffering as a way to experience greater intimacy with God. His dark night of the soul, indeed, became an ecstatic experience: "For I know well the spring that flows and runs, although it is night."

Light a candle, and sit in front of it without speaking for ten minutes. Then, softly speak the prayer below:

And Here's What You Can Say:

Dear Saint John of the Cross,
Help me find the stillness
and the silence
Within this dark night
So that I may sleep calmly
and peacefully
And awake with a joyful heart.

Saint John of the Cross's Feast Day is December 14.

Listening to Saint Antony of Padua

Missing Objects

Sending Out a Saint A.P.B.

*Nothing that grieves us
can be called little: by the eternal laws
of proportion a child's loss of a doll
and a king's loss of a crown
are events of the same size.*
—Mark Twain

*I*f you've ever broken out in a cold sweat because you've lost your car keys, your favorite earring, or (you fear) your honor, don't worry, there are saints who intercede in such matters.

You might notice that the way to get the attention of these particular heavenly hosts seems distressing like, well, blackmail. Of course, no one ever said that supplicants had to be especially kind to those they venerated. So you may find yourself stooping to some of the more mean-spirited tricks that have been used over the centuries to manipulate these saints into action.

When something is lost, no matter how trivial the object, **Antony of Padua** is the saint that all Catholics—whether they call themselves practicing, lapsed, or "recovering"—turn to first. Just ask around. You'll be amazed how many of your friends know about this one.

Antony was born in 1195 in Lisbon, Portugal, and joined the Franciscan order in 1221. He had a reputation for being sickly and not terribly adept at the social graces. No one was surprised when he was not given a public posting but was instead banished to the lonely hermitage of San Paoli, in Italy. However, miracles began being ascribed to him, including one that helped his public-speaking persona. When inhabitants of a nearby town refused to listen to him while he preached, he went to the seaside, with much better luck. "And, truly, it was a marvelous thing to see, how an infinite number of fishes, great and little, lifted their heads above water and listened attentively to the sermon."

Soon Saint Antony became known for his extraordinary powers of eloquence. Despite being described in literature as "undersized and inclined to corpulence," Saint Antony achieved a reputation as a magnetic personality. People crowded into churches and town squares, and anywhere else he appeared. "Hardened criminals, careless folk, and heretics alike" were converted.

At thirty-two, Antony found himself in Padua. His effect on the city was said to be "magical." People who hadn't spoken to each other in years became fast friends; families healed long-standing breaches; thieves repented of their misdeeds. Antony forced the local legislature to pass the first bankruptcy protection law: If people in debt agreed to sell all their belongings, they did not have to go to prison.

One of the most popular of the patron saints, Saint Antony is frequently painted holding the infant Jesus because of a story (first told after his death) that someone saw him through a window holding the young Christ in his arms, "gazing at him with joyful rapture." (This seems to be the basis for the Central American ritual of separating the Christ Child from Saint Antony in order to request intercession on a particular favor.) As the writer of the world's first bankruptcy protection laws, Saint Antony is also patron of the poor. When money or food or clothes are given to the poor in Saint Antony's name, they have historically been called "Saint Antony's bread."

One story told about Saint Antony relates how a young novice in Padua stole a valuable psalter (psalm book) Saint Antony was reading. He prayed for its recovery and the novice was compelled by "an alarming apparition" to return to the scene of his crime and give back the stolen item. No one has ever been clear what was so alarming about the apparition, yet for centuries Saint Antony has been appealed to for finding lost objects.

Here's What You Can Say:

Dear Saint Antony, come around Something's lost and can't be found.

And Here's What You Can Do:

This is a little complicated. Still, our Central American friends swear by it. Your job is to taunt poor Saint Antony into doing what you wish. First, find a picture of Saint Antony. A reproduction of a painting will do. So will a statue. Then, find a picture of the Christ Child. (Again, this can be a reproduction of a painting, or a statue.) Place the two pictures (or statues) next to each other. Make sure Saint Antony can see the Christ Child. Tell Saint Antony what you want from him. Then take the Christ Child away from him. Be resolute! Do not weaken, no matter how sad Saint Antony looks! You must withhold the Christ Child from Saint Antony until your wish is granted. Then, put them back together for at least twenty-four hours to thank Saint Antony for his help.

Italian-American version:

Tony, Tony come around
Something's lost and can't be found.

Bonus Ritual (II)!

Yet another variation on a theme:

Dear Saint Antony, I pray
Bring it back, without delay.

Saint Antony of Padua (Feast Day: June 14),
is also patron saint of the poor and is known as
"the miracle worker."

Saint Phanourios is less well known than Saint Antony in the West, but considered the Eastern Orthodox patron saint of lost articles.

No one knows much about this saint. An icon containing his image was found in a church on the Greek island of Rhodes, along with a manuscript that indicated he had been greatly grieved during his lifetime by the refusal of his mother to convert to Christianity. Over the centuries, Greeks have sought—and received—his help in finding lost or missing objects by praying for the soul of his mother. The more you pray for her, the harder Saint Phanourios will work on your behalf. So sincerity counts.

Here's What You Can Do:

Bake a cake, any kind. Even Duncan Hines will do. This is called a Phanouropita, or cake for Saint Phanourios (which in turn comes from the Greek word *phanerona*, which translates to "I reveal"). Just before you place the cake in the oven, say the following prayer for Saint Phanourios's help. Most important, reassure him that you will pray for the soul of his mother, a very troubled woman. In the morning, you must share the cake with at least seven other people. But do not reveal what you are trying to find, or your request will be denied. Note the operative word "share." Since you have to eat the cake too, you might want to put a little extra effort into baking it. (Some saints don't require that the cakes and breads you bake as offerings are actually consumed—but Saint Phanourios is said to be very vigilant on this point.)

And Here's What You Can Say:

Saint Phanourios,

May your mother be blessed

with eternal peace

As you come to my aid.

Saint Phanourios's Feast Day is unknown.

Saint Thomas

School Stress

When a Little Learning Is a Dangerous Thing

Examinations, sir,
are pure humbug from beginning to end.
If a man is a gentleman,
he knows quite enough,
and if he is not a gentleman,
whatever he knows is bad for him.
—Oscar Wilde

Education: That which discloses
to the wise and disguises from the foolish
their lack of understanding.
—Ambrose Bierce

All of us have been there, and many of us still are. Nothing logs more hours on the worrier's time clock than those pre-exam days and nights. Even those of us who have put the schoolroom decades behind can still wake up sweating from *that dream*— you know, the one in which you haven't studied and are racing from room to room in search of your class. Happily, the heavens are full of saintly scholars, some of whom have a special calling to help those of us who are exam-impaired.

Saint Thomas Aquinas was considered a dunce by all who knew him. But he eventually got the last laugh on those who voted him Least Likely to Succeed by turning into a great scholar. He went on to become the patron saint of students.

Thomas Aquinas's family was a motley collection of bad eggs. Rich and important, they wanted Thomas to indulge in the sensory pleasures of their world, as per family tradition. Instead young Thomas yearned for the monastic life. His mother, the formidable Countess Theodora (think *Dynasty*; think Joan Collins), was so appalled that she had her seventeen-year-old son kidnapped and locked in the family tower. His rough-and-ready brothers sent in a stark-naked prostitute to tempt him into earthly delights. Thomas chased the terrified woman from the room with a firebrand. (The otherwise gentle Thomas's rather hostile attitude toward women can perhaps be traced to this unfortunate experience.) Two angels then appeared with a mystical chastity belt that would henceforth protect Thomas from sexual trauma.

"Sorrow can be abbreviated by good sleep, a bath, and a glass of wine," is one of his bon mots. Unfortunately, so is "because there is a higher water content in women, they are more easily seduced by sexual pleasure."

Thomas's family finally allowed him to pursue his scholarly interests. Although universally described in literature as a fat, quiet, and slow child—so dreamy and preoccupied that he was called "the dumb ox" by his classmates—he went on to earn a doctorate at the University of Paris, and to publish philosophical works and scriptural commentary. He remains one of the most influential theologians and philosophers the Church has ever known. His two great works— *Summa contra Gentiles* and *Summa Theologica* —constitute a systematic exposition of theology long considered a classic of enlightened thought.

Saint Thomas was so immersed in the intellectual life that even a state dinner given by King Louis IX could not keep him anchored in reality. At one point in the meal, Aquinas suddenly pounded the table and shouted, "And that settles the Manichees!" After many years of being taunted and ignored, Thomas Aquinas was declared a Doctor of the Church in 1567—the Church's highest intellectual honor. No surprise he is on call to help students—or anyone facing an exam or other intellectual hurdle.

He also achieved what every student hopes for. When asked what he was most grateful to God for, he replied, "I have understood every page I ever read."

Blessed Saint Thomas, Please listen
to my plea.

I elicit your help to make sure that
my memory does not fail me, and
that my nerves stay calm, so that I
may be successful in my exam.

I trust in your influence,
O Blessed Saint Thomas.

And Here's What You Can Do:

ℱast for twenty-four hours before the exam. During this time, place seven red flowers and as many candles as exam subjects before a picture of Saint Thomas. Light the candles and let them burn, then wrap their remains in a white cloth. Bring this in your pocket to the test. Before leaving, say the above prayer. (Carry nutritious snacks in case the fasting hurts, rather than helps, your testing abilities.)

If you are successful, thank Saint Thomas by giving a poor child some clothes, toys, or food.

Saint Thomas Aquinas (Feast Day: January 28) is also the patron saint of chastity, colleges, and pencil makers.

Saint Gregory the Great is the patron saint of teachers, and of schoolchildren, which makes him quite the diplomat, since he needs to respond to opposing requests for intercession.

Born in A.D. 540 to a wealthy Roman politician, Gregory was one of the most influential writers on Christianity in the early days of the Church. He had a successful civil service career until the age of thirty, when he discovered his religious vocation. At this point he sold all of his possessions and turned his family home into a monastery. He eventually was chosen to succeed Pope Pelaguis as pontiff. In his busy lifetime Gregory founded seven monasteries in Italy and traveled all over the world, spreading the Christian word and giving generously to the poor. He is especially beloved for his contributions to the liturgy of the Mass.

One of the most learned men in the history of the Church, Gregory was extraordinarily committed to extending the intellectual scope of the liturgy as well as its musical beauty. He remains one of just four Doctors of the Latin Church. He also took progressive postures on the issues of the day, answering, for example, the question of whether a woman should receive communion during her menstrual periods, "Why may not one who suffers nature's courses be permitted to enter the Church of God?" he asked.

Here's What You Can Do:

For teachers or students who need Saint Gregory's help:

Decorate a branch or stick with ribbons and crepe paper streamers, and hang it in your bedroom. Before you go to sleep at night, tell someone (or say aloud to yourself) three things you have learned recently.

And Here's What You Can Say:

Saint Gregory,
doctor and scholar,
Bestow your blessings on me
in school today.

Bake something sweet (cake or cookies) and share them with others. Say the preceding prayer to yourself.

Saint Gregory (Feast Day: September 3) is also the patron saint of musicians and singers.

Saint Elmo's Fire

Heavenly House Calls

A Truly Holistic Approach to Good Health

Measure your health by your sympathy
with morning and spring.
If there is no response in you to the
awakening of nature — if the prospect
of an early morning walk
does not banish sleep,
if the warble of the first bluebird does not
thrill you — know that the morning and
spring of your life are past. Thus
may you feel your pulse.
— Henry David Thoreau

If you have health concerns—for yourself or a loved one—whether it's a toothache or something more serious, don't hesitate to find the appropriate patron saint. Saints have traditionally worked miracles with healing the sick and have been invoked for centuries against disease and ill health. (We also recommend choosing the right HMO and seeking modern medical care whenever appropriate.)

Saint James the Greater proves himself to be a powerful ally for anyone who suffers from arthritis, rheumatism, or other bodily aches.

James was one of the twelve apostles, the brother of John, and one of the three witnesses of Christ's agony in the garden of Gethsemane. Jesus had a special name for James and John—"Boanerges," meaning "sons of thunder." Scholars have interpreted this as a personality trait—that the brothers possessed impetuous characters and fiery tempers. Indeed, there are a number of reports that James was not a meek follower: he and John once asked Jesus if they would be allowed to sit on either side of him when he came into glory—anticipating that he would achieve a position of power on earth. The other apostles were shocked that this sort of bold request would be made, but Jesus merely asked James and John if they would drink of the same cup he was going to drink from. They eagerly said yes, not realizing that Jesus meant something quite different from earthly glory. Jesus then told them they would get their wish—meaning, join him in his struggles and eventual martyrdom.

James has long been associated with healing and shells. One legend has it that as a boat containing Saint James's dead body was being taken to Spain for burial, a man on horseback plunged into the sea and began swimming toward the boat. Although it's unclear whether this action was an act of devotion or was an accident, both man and horse came out of the water safely—although covered with scallops. In the Middle Ages, a trip to Saint James's shrine in Santiago de Compostela to commemorate this mysterious man on horseback was considered a holy pilgrimage, and pilgrims often wore shells sewn onto their clothes. To help the pilgrims reach their goal, local townspeople would build shrines out of seashells by the roadside. Wealthier pilgrims were expected to leave money in these shrines for the poorer pilgrims to take. Various reports circulated of arthritis, gout, goiter, or rheumatism sufferers who were cured by touching these roadside seashell shrines.

Here's What You Can Do:

Create a Saint James grotto using whatever shells you can find or buy (although scallop shells are best). Light a candle.

Saint James,

who knew the power of the sea

And was fiery with passion

Grant us the protection

of your intercession

To heal and soothe my body.

Odd Saint Fact:

The roadside grotto practice made it across the English Channel where you can still see Saint James's grottoes by English roadsides. An old English children's rhyme (used to beg for pennies) commemorates this:

Please to remember the Grotto

It's only once a year

Father's gone to sea

Mother's gone to fetch him back

So please remember me.

Saint James the Greater's Feast Day is July 25.

Saint Agatha was a woman ahead of her time. For centuries she has been invoked against diseases of the breast, long before "breast cancer awareness" received appropriate medical, political, or social attention.

orn circa A.D. 200 in Sicily, Agatha was yet another beautiful, chaste, and strongly resolute woman who was fiercely determined to remain a virgin for the sake of Jesus Christ. Agatha resisted numerous attacks on her virginity and faith, most notably the advances of a high Sicilian official, Quintian, who took her to court in an attempt to force her to renounce her Christianity. Rather than succumb, Agatha prayed aloud in front of the judge, saying to God, "I am your sheep; make me worthy to overcome the devil." Quintian had her locked in a brothel, where she was repeatedly raped. Still, she refused to give in to him. A persistent wretch, Quintian tortured her by every means at his disposal, then threw her into prison. As Agatha lay dying, her last words were a prayer in which she thanked God for giving her the patience to suffer. Oy!

One of the tortures inflicted on poor Agatha as she was being stretched out on the rack was having her breasts slowly sliced off her body. Her response? She said quietly to the offending soldiers (servants of the dastardly Quintian), "But didn't your mother nourish you with these?" Later that night, Saint Peter appeared to Agatha in her cell and offered her a heavenly ointment that miraculously restored her body to health.

Here's What You Can Do:

Bake small loaves of bread shaped like breasts. Choose any recipe you like, as long as the dough can be shaped and will retain its shape while being baked. These are called "Agathas." Distribute your Agathas to people you love (and who love you) and ask them to pray to Agatha to intercede on your behalf.

Odd Saint Fact:

The apparent reason for Agatha's long-standing association with baked goods is that as she was often portrayed in medieval paintings carrying her breasts on a plate, some of the less quick-witted believers thought she was carrying loaves of bread. On her feast day, it is still traditional in Eastern Europe for loaves of bread to be blessed at Mass and distributed to the sick in the parish.

Saint Agatha's Feast Day is February 5. She can also be invoked against earthquakes and fires.

There really was a *Saint Elmo*. He is revered because he frequently intercedes on behalf of children and infants who suffer from colic or other stomach ailments, and because of his willingness to protect sailors against sudden storms.

Erasmus, more popularly known as Elmo, was a Syrian bishop circa A.D. 300 who repeatedly fled persecution, only to be caught, tortured, rescued, caught again . . . you get the idea. His first escape from bloodthirsty anti-Christians took him to Mount Lebanon, where he secluded himself in a remote cave—and had his meals brought to him by a friendly raven. The emperor Diocletian, determined to smoke out all renegade Christians, eventually found him there and had him rolled in pitch and set afire. After being rescued by an angel, Elmo fled to a hermitage in Illyricum, but he was soon captured, thrown in prison, and tortured, eventually dying a noble martyr's death. Some medieval legends say Elmo was one of the Fourteen Holy Helpers,* a

*The Fourteen Holy Helpers were a group of saints popular in Germany in the fourteenth, fifteenth, and sixteenth centuries. (The cult

group of saints particularly venerated for their ability to bring spiritual solace to the dying.

Elmo's reputation as patron of sailors, and a protector against storms, comes from a story that says he continued preaching the word of God, undeterred by a fierce tempest. One version of the legend even has him miraculously unharmed after being struck by lightning. The eerie blue light (due to electrical discharge) that sometimes hovers around ship mastheads after a storm is over is called "St. Elmo's fire." It's a sign that Saint Elmo has been hard at work, and that all will be well.

Elmo's reputation as a powerful intermediary against childhood stomach ailments is now considered the result of a simple error. The sailing navigation instrument that artists frequently depict Elmo holding is called a windlass. At one point, the faithful mistook it for an instrument of torture—leading to the story that one of Elmo's many sufferings for Christ involved having his intestines carved out while he was still alive. Still, Elmo seems to have valiantly taken up this patronage despite the erroneous origins of this association.

spread to Hungary and Sweden but then died out before reaching the rest of then-Europe.) These saints were usually invoked as a protection against illness, and on deathbeds—particularly if the dying individual had not led an exemplary life. Although the members of this group varied, it usually included Acacius, Barbara, Blaise, Catherine of Alexandria, Christopher, Cyricus, Denis, Erasmus (Elmo), Eustace. George, Giles, Margaret of Antioch, Pantaleon, and Vitus. Sometimes Antony. Nicolas, or Roch would be substituted for one of the above.

Here's What You Can Do:

For a child or infant suffering from stomach ailments:

Light a candle and place it by the ailing child or infant (but out of his/her reach, of course). Rub the child's belly gently.

And Here's What You Can Say:

Saint Elmo, help release this innocent one from suffering.

Bonus Ritual!

If worried about the effect of a possible storm while on water:

Light a candle, and place it in a prominent place in the boat or ship. (If a candle is impossible, a small lamp, flashlight, or even match will do.) Place as high as possible, hopefully above the heads of the other inhabitants of the vessel.

Say the following prayer: Saint Elmo, preserve us from all dangerous effects of this storm.

Odd Saint Fact:

According to Greek superstition, Saint Elmo's fire is a portent of evil to come, but disaster can be averted by pulling on a pig's tail.

Saint Elmo's Feast Day is June 2.

Saint Apollonia has long been invoked by people who suffer from toothache. Don't delay in making that emergency appointment with your dentist, but try asking Apollonia for some interim relief.

Saint Apollonia lived in the first century in Alexandria, Egypt. Saint Dionysius first recorded the story of an elderly virgin who refused to renounce her faith despite being taunted by lusty young pagans. First her nasty tormentors pulled out all her teeth one by one. When that failed to have any effect, they threatened to burn her alive unless she recited blasphemous sayings in the public square. Without hesitation, Apollonia leaped into the flames and was instantly martyred.

We call upon Saint Apollonia for tooth problems because of the dramatic way in which she suffered.

Many medieval portraits of Saint Apollonia depict her holding pincers with a tooth in its grip, or wearing a necklace with a single tooth as ornament. Later legends transformed her into a beautiful young girl—a king's daughter—who is tortured by having her teeth extracted. In this version, she still refused to yield, and was martyred, but not before promising to help toothache sufferers who call upon her for aid.

Here's What You Can Do:

Write the following on three separate pieces of paper:

Dear Saint Apollonia, intercede on my behalf.

Place the papers in your pocket, and carry them for twenty-four hours. At the end of that time, light a candle and burn the papers one by one in the flame.

And Here's What You Can Say:

Dear Saint Apollonia, Healer of toothaches, Take away my suffering.

Bonus Ritual!

Buy (or make) a replica of a tooth and hang it around your neck for at least twenty-four hours.

Saint Apollonia's Feast Day is February 9.

Don't throw away that Motrin or Tylenol (or whatever does the trick for you), but try Saint Denis if you suffer from headaches.

S aint Denis is probably a composite of several early martyrs, and has been variously mistaken for other early saints such as Dionysius, a disciple of

Saint Paul, as well as a philosopher now called Pseudo-Dionysius (it does get confusing). But the most commonly accepted Denis story says he was sent to Gaul (France) from Italy around A.D. 200 along with five other holy pilgrims to convert the pagans found in abundance there. After establishing a mission near the Seine—on the site that later became Paris—Denis was captured by the pagans, and, with two of his fellow missionaries, imprisoned and finally beheaded.

Denis soon proved his saintly hardheadedness. He simply got up off the floor, picked up his head, and walked (or should we say stumbled?) six miles to the site that now houses the famous French abbey of Saint-Denis. Hence his reputation of being eager to help anyone who suffers from headaches, even those of the most grievous kind. (He is frequently depicted in art as upright and otherwise healthy-looking except that he is carrying his head under his arm.) According to the legend, when asked upon reaching the abbey about the most difficult part of his journey, his head replied, "The first step."

A different, and probably more reputable, spin on the Denis legend says his decapitated body was thrown into the Seine, but later retrieved and buried by his followers at a nearby church, which later became the abbey of Saint-Denis. The remains are there to this day.

Here's What You Can Do:

℘lace a handful of rose petals in a wooden bowl. Dip a soft cloth in the water and press to your forehead.

And Here's What You Can Say:

Saint Denis, who suffered
in silence,
hear our voices as we ask for your
intercession,
liberate us from this headache.

Saint Denis's Feast Day is October 9. Saint Denis is also the patron saint of Paris and of France, and he can be invoked against fear and frenzy.

When stress has gotten you down to the point where you suffer physical symptoms — especially headaches and chest pains — we recommend appealing to Saint Teresa of Avila (but also call your doctor if symptoms persist).

This much-beloved saint was born in 1515 of a wealthy Spanish family, whose place in society was precarious. Her grandfather was a *converso*, or Spanish Jew who was forced to convert to Christianity during the Inquisition. Teresa showed her inclination for the spiritual life early on. As a child, she didn't play with dolls. Instead, she and her brother pretended to be missionaries. They created elaborate fantasies that always ended up with a grand finale of both being gloriously "martyred" for Christ.

Teresa's mother died when she was just fourteen, and soon after, her father sent her away to be educated by Augustine nuns. Upon her arrival at the convent, Teresa fell severely ill and almost died. After a period of intense prayer and meditation that accompanied her slow recovery to health. Teresa began having visions. An angel showed Teresa an empty space in hell amidst the tortured souls, and said, "This is for you if you don't change your life." Teresa became convinced that God was calling her.

At the age of twenty Teresa took her vows, and became a part of the Carmelite community at Avila, which was a surprisingly liberal and social one: the townspeople mixed freely with the nuns, and there were constant parties and social engagements. As Teresa was pretty, charming, and witty, she was a great favorite with everyone both inside and outside the convent walls. One phrase attributed to her is "God preserve us from stupid nuns!" At another time, "I have no defense against affection," Teresa said. "I could be bribed with a sardine." Eventually, however, she became disillusioned with the frivolity and social orientation of her order, and embarked on what would be a lifelong study of the power of silent prayer and meditation.

After immersing herself in the lives and works of other penitents who eventually spurned the ways of the world—particularly Mary Magdalene and Saint Augustine—Teresa began having odd mystical visions and ecstatic seizures so severe—and public— that she became rather notorious.

Teresa was mocked, thought ridiculous—and even openly condemned for increasingly erratic behavior related to her mystical visions. Finally, in the hopes of stemming the episodes, Teresa was ordered by her Mother Superior to write her experiences down. She proved to have a keen observing eye and a talent for concise and thoughtful analyses of complex theological issues. Her personal journals turned into renowned religious writings, including her most famous publication, *The Interior Castle.*

Teresa often struggled with health issues; she became seriously ill for the second time shortly after taking her formal vows. She was so sick, in fact, that she had to leave her religious community and return to her father's house, where she stayed three years until she regained her strength. (She later attributed her return to health to an appeal to Saint Joseph.) Her rigorous self-discipline for silence and peaceful solitude provide an infinitely practical model for anyone suffering from stress, headaches, or heart disease.

After twenty-five years with the Carmelites, Teresa left to found her own religious house in order to create a contemplative lifestyle more compatible with her views of spiritual growth. (So extremely basic were considered the habits of this new order that they became known as the shoeless Carmelites—even though they did allow themselves to wear sandals made of rough hemp.)

These "reformed" Carmelites took strict vows of poverty, solitude, and simplicity; by the end of Teresa's life, there were seventeen convents advocating her uniquely simplified view of religious life.

Because of her writings and scholarship, she was declared a Doctor of the Church after her death.

$\mathcal{T}$ake off your shoes. Light five candles, place them near a picture of Saint Teresa, and repeat her most famous prayer.

And Here's What You Can Say:

Let nothing disturb thee

Let nothing dismay thee

All things pass

God never changes

Patience attains

All that is strived for

He who has God

Finds he lacks nothing.

Saint Teresa of Avila's Feast Day is October 15.

Trying to conceive? Worried about having a safe pregnancy? Turn to Saint Gerard Majella, that most gentle gentlemanly saint.

*B*orn in Italy in 1726, Gerard began his adult life as a tailor, but he sold his shop and entered a Franciscan convent when he was twenty-three.

Although he desperately wanted to be a priest, he was turned down because of his poor health (Gerard died of consumption before his thirtieth birthday), and so had to be content with the title of "lay brother"—the lowest rank on the religious order totem pole—which he attained when he was twenty-six. As a lay brother, he acted in a menial capacity, first as a tailor, then a gardener, and finally a porter for the other, more important monks on the monastery. And Gerard would have vanished from history if he hadn't discovered remarkable powers for healing and prophecy. He found he could read others' thoughts, as well as levitate and bilocate (that's the ability to be in two physically separate places simultaneously).

Apparently, Gerard was so kind, gentle, and trustworthy that women felt comfortable around him. (He had grown up with three sisters.)

For his ability to intercede for would-be parents, Gerard has been called "the most famous wonder worker of the eighteenth century," and we know of at least one twentieth-century woman who asked Saint Gerard for help in conceiving; she went on to have five healthy sons and named each of them ... you guessed it: Gerard.

One story about why he was considered especially friendly toward pregnant women says that after he entered the monastery, a local woman accused him of "lewd behavior" toward her (we're not quite sure what this meant in the eighteenth century, although we can probably guess). He refused to challenge her statement, or attempt to refute her; later, she admitted she had lied. (Sorry, that's as specific as it gets.) Gerard's mother stood by him, insisting to anyone who would listen that her beloved only son was "born for heaven."

Here's What You Can Do:

Sit down in a comfortable chair, fold your hands on your lap, and close your eyes for ten minutes.

And Here's What You Can Say:

Saint Gerard,

Your devotion to the infant Jesus

has given thee special influence in

pleading the causes of all mothers

We implore thee to intercede for those among us who look forward to the glory of motherhood.

Protector of expectant mothers, preserve me from danger and excessive pain in childbirth. Shield this child I now carry.

Saint Gerard's Feast Day is October 16.

If you have a sore throat, or problems with your thyroid, or any other illness or disease in the neck area, Saint Blaise is your spiritual physician.

Saint Blaise was a fourth-century Armenian about whom few actual facts are known. Although a number of fictional "biographies" of Blaise's life have circulated throughout the centuries, none is believed to be authentic. Here's what we do know: He was the son of wealthy Christians. He was consecrated bishop of Sebastea at an extraordinarily young age, and subsequently fell victim to one of Emperor Licinius's periodic persecutions of Christians.

Blaise has long been revered throughout Eastern Europe as one of the Fourteen Holy Helpers, or special saints deemed particularly efficacious for aiding in times of sickness, or in assuring eternal salvation for the dying.

There are numerous Blaise legends about his miraculous healing powers. These powers were first demonstrated as he hid from his persecutors in a cave and cured sick animals belonging to the local peasants. To this day, farmers in Eastern Europe bless newly born or newly purchased cattle in Blaise's name.

Blaise, like Saint Francis, apparently had a calming influence on wild beasts. One story has him eloquently convincing a wolf that it didn't *really* want to eat the pig it was carrying between its jaws. The wolf released the pig (much to the relief of the pig's owner, and the pig, we imagine), and spent the rest of its life following Blaise around like a pet dog.

Another legend explains Blaise's connection with ailments of the throat. When he was being led to his death through crowded streets, he witnessed a young boy choking on a fishbone (from his pre-execution-watching lunch, we guess). Blaise managed to escape from his captors long enough to give the boy the spiritual version of the Heimlich maneuver. Being a saint, he then of course returned quietly to his guards and was beheaded on schedule. In a different, less dramatic version, a woman brings her choking son to Blaise's cave, where the boy is duly saved.

Even though Saint Blaise's feast day, February 3, is not a "holy day of obligation"—that is, Catholics are not required to go to Mass on that day—it's still a big draw; many parishioners still show up at Mass on that morning specifically to have their throats blessed by the priest and to ask for Saint Blaise's protection in the coming year. Typically, the priest will cross two blessed candles at the throat of each supplicant, saying, "Through the intercession of Saint Blaise, Bishop and martyr, may God deliver you from illness of the throat and from every other evil. In the name of the Father, Son, and of the Holy Spirit. Amen."

Here's What You Can Do:

*B*ake some Saint Blaise bread, which is ordinary bread shaped into long, thin loaves. You need to make at least two loaves, and you can use your standard recipe, or frozen dough, or the trusty bread machine. If you're *really* rushed for time, just go out and buy some breadsticks.

You can also use candles in place of the bread.

Then, light a separate votive candle—beeswax is best—and cross the breadsticks or (unlit) candles at the base of your throat.

Saint Blaise,

Pray for me

Command that this obstruction

Go up or come down

Deliver me from illnesses

of the throat

And from every other evil.

Once you have completed the prayer, you should eat the bread and drink hot tea steeped with honey while the beeswax candle remains burning.

Odd Saint Fact:

Here's a gruesome footnote to Blaise's death: He was supposedly shredded alive by wool combs—painfully sharp instruments used when preparing recently shorn sheep wool for weaving—before having his head cut off. This is why Blaise is frequently depicted carrying a wool comb as his emblem.

Saint Blaise's Feast Day is February 3.

Saint Anne is a versatile saint who can be appealed to by women wanting a husband; by infertile women wanting to conceive; and by pregnant women who want to experience a safe and peaceful childbirth.

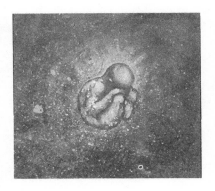

Anne, or Hannah, means "grace." This devout Jewish housewife had given up on having children—she was well past menopause—when she finally conceived the child she'd been longing for. It turned out to be Mary, the future mother of Jesus. Not much is known about Anne, although various legends say, alternately, that she was married three times, or that she and her first husband, Joachim, Mary's father, had prayed for a child for many years before God relented.

Although she was ignored for many centuries, interest in Saint Anne sprang up with the renewed cult of Mary in the twelfth century, and Anne has since gained a strong reputation for imparting wisdom and equanimity to those who appeal to her.

Numerous folk legends associate Anne with interceding on behalf of women for all sorts of problems. Her miraculous conception of Mary so late in life makes her an obvious source of hope for women wanting to conceive; and in general she is seen as a model for anyone in emotional turmoil.

Here's What You Can Do:

Light a candle on a Tuesday evening (through the ages, for reasons unknown, Tuesday has come to be closely associated with Saint Anne). Place a picture of Saint Anne near it, and let it burn all night.

And Here's What You Can Say:

For conceiving a child, or for a safe childbirth:

Saint Anne, give me grace
and strength
Grant me courage and
a quiet mind
May I be brave, constant,
and serene

And help me be loyal and loving to
all who enter my life.

For centuries, Englishwomen have invoked Saint
Anne for help in finding husbands by reciting the following couplet:

Dear Saint Anne,

Send me a man.

Odd Saint Fact:

Saint Anne's patronage over matters of fertility
even extends to the soil. In some parts of Europe,
much-needed rain is known as "Saint Anne's dowry."

Saint Anne's Feast Day is July 26.

You can turn to Saint Brigid when you don't quite feel yourself, and need a general pick-me-up in the health department.

$\mathcal{B}$rigid (also known as Bridget, Bride, or, more affectionately, Bridey), rivals Saint Patrick for premier saint status in Ireland. Her ability to intercede with God for special favors is legendary.

Brigid was born near Dundalk, in Louth, around A.D. 450. Her father was a pagan chieftain, her mother, one of his slaves—and from the time she could walk Brigid was treated as little more than a slave herself. One of her many chores was taking care of her father's cows. One Brigid legend says that as they did the milking together, her pagan mother whispered to her what little she knew about the strange new Christian faith spreading throughout Ireland. Brigid was so struck by what she heard that she sought out Saint Patrick and asked to be baptized. Her father, naturally, was not pleased. He did all the usual nasty things that fathers of saints did (tried to marry her off to a pagan; tried forcing her to renounce her faith, etc., etc.), but Brigid stood firm. When she finally escaped her father's clutches, she moved to Kildare, established a monastery, and continued her life's work of helping the poor and the sick, and spreading the holy word throughout Ireland.

Brigid delighted in wreaking havoc on the social and religious status quo. There are many Brigid-as-subversive stories: One has her giving away her father's entire herd of cows—and many of his other worldly goods as well—to the local poor (he was furious); another has her living in a cave and doling out the various dairy products she concocted from friendly cows who came obediently to her to be milked (the cows' owners also were not pleased). Another legend has her changing her bathwater into beer so some wandering evangelists could quench their thirst. Once, when an especially illustrious group of holy men happened by, Brigid was distressed that she had nothing to feed them, but when she prayed to God, her cows spouted so much milk that an entire lake was formed. (It's still there, and still called The Lake of Milk.) Another persistent rumor is that she and Saint Ibor—a contemporary holy colleague—got drunk one night, and amid the celebration, Ibor consecrated Brigid as a bishop.

There are numerous stories of Brigid's miraculous ability to heal the sick or dying, and she is especially useful in the case of minor aches and pains, such as toothaches, stomachaches, headaches, and earaches. Pilgrims still flock to her altar at Kildare to be cured of various illnesses. According to legend, when Brigid finally took her vows to become a nun, the wooden altar came to life, sprouting leaves and flowers, and to this day retains magical healing properties. A fire is still carefully tended in the chapel at Kildare; legend says it has burned continuously since the day Brigid died. For centuries, the fire was guarded at all times by a cadre of twenty formidable nuns (presumably they took shifts, like the guards at Buckingham Palace). They also planted bushes in a circle around the flames and forbade any men to enter. Saint Brigid's shrine is now, however, an equal opportunity place of worship. The fire represents Brigid's enduring love, steadfastness, and—yes—stubbornness, as well as her joyful endurance of a life that encompassed much hardness and strife.

Here's What You Can Do:

Weave a Saint Brigid's cross (directions below) and display it in a prominent place in your house for a speedy "return to health." Although this cross is traditionally made of straw, you can use strips of paper, strips of cardboard, or any other handy material, by taking 16 pieces of equal length, and weaving them together. You can also make one to wear as a pin or a necklace, or make two as a pair of earrings.

Here's how you make a Saint Brigid's cross: Take 16 pieces of straw of equal length (they should be at least

6 inches long). Fold the first piece of straw in half. Then fold the second piece in half, and hook it *through* the fold of the first piece. Fold a third piece in half, and hook it *over* the second piece. Continue adding pieces of straw that have been folded in half, making sure to hook each piece *over* the piece you had just previously placed. When you are finished using all 16 straws, tie the loose ends with a piece of twine. The result should look like the diagram on page 114.

And Here's What You Can Say:

Brigid, inspire me with your life

Give me a healthy heart,

mind, and body

So I may strive after and attain

The true riches of the world.

Odd Saint Fact:

You can find one of Brigid's alleged shoes—improbable, considering her penchant for poverty—made of silver and sparkling with precious jewels—in the National Museum in Dublin.

Saint Brigid's Feast Day is February 1. She is also patron saint of fugitives. So keep Bridey in mind if you have to go underground for any reason.

If you're worried about your eyesight, or perhaps are just having a bad eyeglass or contacts day, try asking Saint Lucy for her help.

Saint Lucy is a fourth-century maiden about whom facts are scarce. Each Lucy legend has an appealingly dramatic Perils-of-Pauline plotline— with the appropriate happy ending (if you're focused on heavenly, as opposed to earthly, rewards, that is).

As best we can tell, Lucy was born in Sicily in A.D. 300 or so. One legend claims she rejected a wealthy suitor. He threw a fit, dragged her into court, and accused Lucy of ... Christianity. Hey, if the shoe fits.

Lucy was martyred in an appropriately gruesome way. First the local pagan authorities tried the usual trick of hauling her off to a brothel (apparently these persecutors had no imagination), but she miraculously couldn't be moved, even by the strongest Sicilians in the neighborhood, as she "had become as heavy as a mountain." Then they tried setting her on fire, but she proved inflammable. Finally, they resorted successfully to the sword and finally managed to kill her.

Why the association with eyes? Good question. One version of the legend says that Lucy's eyes were torn out as part of the tormenting that led to her martyrdom.

Another Lucy story (which contradicts the other one) says that one of her many admirers was so much in love with her that he couldn't sleep for thinking of her beautiful eyes. Lucy took pity on him; she tore out her eyes and sent them to him on a platter. That did it, of course: He became a Christian.

In both versions, however, Lucy's eyes were miraculously restored, which is why Lucy is frequently depicted in art as blooming and unmutilated, even though she is also holding a spare pair of eyes on a platter in front of her. Lucy's name means "light" and has the same Latin root as the word *lucid*.

Here's What You Can Do:

Light a candle. If you can, place a picture of Lucy in front of it (you can find holy cards and other Lucy mementos at any religious supply store—she's very popular). Place tiny replicas of eyes in front of it, and say the following prayer. (A drawing, even a primitive one, of eyes will do fine.)

And Here's What You Can Say:

Lucy, as you did not hide your light
But let it shine for the world to see
Help my own eyes

In this special case
But also to illuminate my life.

Lucy, please give the ability
to see clearly
How I can help others
In my work
While at play
During conversation
And throughout my day.

Odd Saint Fact:

Lucy's body supposedly remains fresh and uncorrupted by decay. It is kept in a tiny church in Naples "near the railway station," as *The Oxford Dictionary of Saints* helpfully points out (no other listing in this venerable reference guide contains such Baedeker-like instructions for would-be pilgrims).

Bonus Ritual!

In Britain, unmarried women appeal to Saint Lucy to show them a vision of their future mates by chanting the following before going to sleep:

Sweet Lucy, let me know
Whose cloth I shall lay
Whose bed I shall make

Whose child I shall bear
Whose darling I shall be.

In Sweden, Saint Lucy is an especially big deal. Her feast day is in mid-December, when the days are short and the nights long. To celebrate Lucy's spiritual luminosity, the youngest girl of the household traditionally arises early, lights candles, and brings fresh-baked cinnamon rolls to everyone.

Saint Lucy's Feast Day is December 13.

Saint George

Guarding the Hearth and Home

Activating Your Own Spiritual Security System

If I were asked to name the chief benefit
of the house, I should say:
the house shelters day-dreaming,
the house protects the dreamer,
the house allows one to dream in peace.
—Gaston Bachelard

You are a king by your own fireside, as
much as any monarch in his throne.
—Miguel de Cervantes

A comfortable house is a great source of
happiness. It ranks immediately after
health and a good conscience.
—Sydney Smith

Worried about burglars? Find yourself obsessing about vandals, infestations of mice, fire hazards, or earthquakes? Or maybe you just want to get a good selling price? Look no further. Here we have a host of saints who specialize in the art of protecting your castle, no matter how humble it might be. Oh, and these saints also include ones who will make sure you have a terrific tomato crop and that your cat or fish stay healthy.

When moving into a new house or apartment, ask Saint George to help make it a comfortable — and safe — place for you to live.

You probably know some version of the legend of the Boy and the Dragon: A particularly nasty dragon periodically swoops down to terrorize a provincial town and the only thing that will stop it is a human sacrifice. Of course, it won't be satisfied unless the victim is a beautiful (and chaste) princess. A local hero of humble origins volunteers to help; he leaps into a grossly mismatched fight with the fire-breathing beast and—naturally—kills the dragon, winning the gratitude of the people and the princess for himself.

And there *was* a real Saint George, although little is known of his life. A soldier by training, he lived in Palestine around A.D. 300. At that time, the Roman emperor Diocletian was in the midst of one of his periodic attempts to purge the Christian faith from his empire (he failed), and George was one of the more notable casualties because of the bravery he demonstrated in battle.

But Saint George's popularity throughout the centuries has very little to do with the actual facts of his life. As so often with the early saints, George's cult rests on a whimsical balance of mythology and reality. (Scholars have pointed out that the supposed Christian story of Saint George is really an adaptation of the Greek—read pagan—legend of Perseus and Andromeda, in which a bold young hero slays a dragon to rescue a beautiful princess. And there have been infinite variations of this legend created by civilizations throughout the ages.)

The Saint George version sticks very close to the original: George still goes to battle to save the girl from the dragon, but—unlike in the original Greek version—refuses to kill the dragon until the king and all his subjects agree to convert to Christianity. (Which they do. Immediately. Trembling.) And, of course, George will have nothing to do with the girl after victory is his, resolutely holding onto his virginity.

Although revered throughout Europe, Saint George is especially popular in England, where his spectacular display of courage against all odds struck an emotional chord. (Coincidentally, he shares the same birthday as another local hero, William Shakespeare.) King Edward III eventually designated him patron saint of the entire country, and English soldiers cried "Saint George!" as they rode into battle. Indeed, the British flag is an adaptation of George's own emblem: a white flag with a red cross embossed on it.

In art (and George has been an immensely popular subject throughout the ages) George always stands ready to protect. He's usually depicted dressed in full knight's armor, holding his flag, either engaged in battle with the dragon or standing victorious above the dead beast.

In England, his feast day is celebrated by a universal displaying of the British flag and the wearing of a red rose.

Here's What You Can Do:

Walk from room to room in your new home carrying an object that symbolizes Saint George. (This can be a picture, a book of his life, a cross, or even the British flag, with its version of Saint George's cross.)

And Here's What You Can Say:

Dear Saint George,

who fought so valiantly,

protect this house/apartment

from all dangers

Physical and spiritual.

Bonus Ritual!

In the Alps, shepherds give lambs to the local church in thanks for Saint George's help keeping their flock safe from wolves and illness in the coming year. While you may not have any lambs to offer, perhaps an appropriate gift to a local charity would also keep George on your side.

To demonstrate just how apocryphal the George legend is considered by Church officials, when English pilgrims visited the chapel of the English College (a small Catholic church in Rome), they supposedly began their prayers by reciting the following:

Point I:
Let us consider we know very little indeed about Saint George.

Point II:
Let us consider that the little we do know is very doubtful.

Point III:
Let us consider that it is quite certain we shall never know anything more about Saint George.

Saint George's Feast Day is April 23.

Saint Gertrude is your heavenly exterminator if your home is plagued with mice, rats, or other unwelcome visitors from the animal or insect kingdom. You might want to keep her picture posted on your refrigerator, or wherever you keep other emergency contact info.

Little is known about Saint Gertrude, except that she was placed in a local Benedictine convent in the late thirteenth century at the tender age of five years in order to be educated. She spent the rest of her life there, studying scriptures and writing five highly respected books of theology.

Gertrude is regarded by scholars as an important medieval mystic, which means she experienced a personal and intimate relationship with God in which they communicated via visions. Gertrude often had her most important conversations with God—that is, her most magnificent visions—during the singing of High Mass. (Gertrude's visions are renowned for emphasizing God's compassion and generosity toward humankind.)

It *is* a bit puzzling how Gertrude came to be associated with eliminating rodents. However, it is still reported that the water from her monastery's well has marvelous effects when sprinkled on doorways or windows of an infested building.

Here's What You Can Do:

Construct a shrine to Saint Gertrude. Don't worry—it can be simple. Start with her picture—draw it yourself if you can't find one—or a small statue or a medal. Then place some replicas of mice or rats near it. Small plastic or rubber ones are good—the kind you can get in a toy shop—but a photo or sketch should work fine. Place some flower petals (roses are best, but whatever blossom is easily available) in a glass of water nearby. Say a silent prayer for Saint Gertrude's help. Then sprinkle the flower-scented water on the doorways and windowsills of the room(s) where you are having your infestation problem.

Traditionally, the mice have been made of gold or silver and sprinkled with holy water, but we'll let you off easy. And don't forget to put rice, flour, sugar, and other temptations in tightly sealed containers *right away.*

Odd Saint Fact:

Gertrude is notable for saying mysteriously (but perhaps wisely), that "it is a fearful mistake to believe that because our wishes are not accomplished they can do no harm."

Saint Gertrude's Feast Day is November 16.

$\mathcal{S}$aint $\mathcal{S}$tephen has a centuries-old reputation for being the best general odd-jobs-man you can get when experiencing problems with your house, garden, or domestic animals.

Stephen was a Greek Jew who converted to Christianity with such fervor that he was subsequently chosen by the apostles to help spread Jesus' teachings throughout the known world. Appointed one of the seven venerable "deacons" of the early Church, Stephen's responsibilities included distributing money to the poor—and converting as many pagans and Jews to the new religion as quickly as possible.

Stephen apparently did the latter with a vengeance, possessing so fiery a tongue and so much chutzpah that his preaching led directly to his death. Ironically, the auspicious way he died (he was stoned) has somehow translated into Stephen's becoming the patron of bricklayers, stonemasons, and home builders.

It makes for a dramatic story. Already on trial for blasphemy (after accusing the Jewish elders of being the murderers of Christ), Stephen stood before the judges and was apparently unable to resist taunting them further. "You are," he said, "stiff-necked and un-circumcised in heart and ears." The attending mob was so enraged by these insults they stormed the court (even before there was time to issue a formal judgment against him) and dragged Stephen outside the city walls, where they stoned him to death.

Stephen has always been an immensely popular saint, but not for reasons that the Church formally approves of. The cult of Saint Stephen is one of the problematic "solstice" cults (those of Saint John the Baptist and Saint Thomas the Apostle are others) because his feast day occurs on December 26, just before the New Year and just after the winter solstice. This was traditionally a very important time for pagan peoples, who supported themselves primarily by agriculture and for whom the beginning of a new harvest cycle was a significant milestone. As Christianity spread, many pagan practices meant to ensure a good harvest and good health in the coming agricultural year (both for humans and for any animals they owned) were conveniently transferred over to Saint Stephen. Stephen was also the first Christian martyr—following Christ of course—and that's another reason his feast day is December 26.

Here's What You Can Say:

Mighty Saint Stephen,
I ask for your protection in the
coming year

For my house and home
For those who reside here
And all others who need your help.

And Here's What You Can Do:

(1) If you want to ask for Saint Stephen's protection for any household pets or animals, bake a loaf of bread (your favorite recipe will do) in the shape of a horseshoe. Give a slice of this bread to every animal you want to protect. (No, they don't actually have to *eat* it. Just place it in their food bowl.)

(2) If you want Saint Stephen to protect your home and its inhabitants (human or otherwise) against illness, disease, hail, or storms (yes, this covers a great deal of ground), place some oats in a bag and hang it prominently in your house, saying the above prayer. Cheerios will work fine.

(3) To ask Saint Stephen to protect your house against evil spirits, walk around it three times. (Traditionally, you would ride your horse, but a brisk stride should do the trick.)

(4) To ask Saint Stephen to protect a loved one against illness, place a few pieces of straw in the appropriate pillowcase while saying the above prayer. (Traditionally, this would be straw taken from a Christmas manger or Nativity scene, and it would have been blessed by a priest.)

Pagan and Christian practices converge in an odd custom that prevailed throughout the medieval world, and which is still practiced in rural parishes in Poland and Hungary. On Saint Stephen's feast day, people bring oats to church to be blessed; once Mass is concluded, the blessed oats are thrown at the priest. This is supposedly done to commemorate Stephen's stoning, but it is also tied to the pagan rituals for ensuring a good harvest in the coming year. (Folklore scholars have also pointed out that this provided a safe "outlet" for local people who wish to punish unpopular clergymen in their communities.)

If you decide to try this, we suggest letting your priest know what you are up to ahead of time, so he isn't unduly surprised when pelted by Cheerios or another modern oat product.

Odd Saint Fact:

Saint Paul, one of early Christianity's most ardent missionaries, was present at Stephen's stoning in his own preconverted state. Known then as the cynical (and pagan) Saul, he not only witnessed Stephen's horrible death but actually cheered the crowd on, going as far as to hold the coats of the perpetrators. Stephen probably had a thing or two to say to him when they met in heaven.

Saint Stephen's Feast Day is December 26.

If you're concerned about protecting your house from vandalism, natural disasters, or the elements—or if you simply want to get a good price when you're ready to sell it, Saint Joseph is your man.

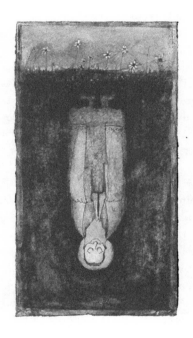

If you take a shovel and start digging in the yards of just about any urban Catholic neighborhood—but certainly the Italian ones—throughout the country, you'll unearth untold numbers of Saint Joseph statues. These come in all shapes and sizes and can be made of metal, plastic, or porcelain—but all have been planted to entreat Joseph for help protecting the home in question, or, more probably, selling it quickly and for a miraculous profit. (It's a wonder Saint Joseph has time for anything else, especially when mortgage rates drop.)

Joseph was, of course, the older carpenter who took on a pregnant teenage bride, and became the stepfather of Jesus. Joseph didn't receive much attention until the first Crusades began, but once the Joseph ball started rolling it didn't stop. Renaissance mystics John of the Cross and Teresa of Avila were especially big fans of Joseph, helping spread the word of his heavenly influence—and his power to intercede for those in trouble—through their writings and preachings.

Soon after Jesus was born, Joseph had a dream that warned him of the impending danger from King Herod, and he fled with his young family into Egypt. Although the facts of his later life are unclear, it is generally believed that Joseph died before his adopted son, Jesus, was crucified. It was Joseph's devotion to his family, and his line of work—he was a carpenter like his son—that caused him to be designated the patron of, respectively, fathers and carpenters.

Indeed, nearly every aspect of Joseph's life has been translated into a special patronage. In addition to carpenters and fathers, Joseph is also patron of laborers, stepfathers, travelers and refugees (think of the flight into Egypt), and also of newly engaged couples.

Many other saints have testified to the efficacy of asking for Saint Joseph's counsel on a wide variety of subjects. Of Joseph's power to successfully intercede on behalf of earthly requests, Teresa of Avila wrote, "I cannot call to mind that I have ever asked him for anything that he has not granted. To other saints Our Lord seems to have given grace to help in some special necessity; but to this glorious saint, I know by experience, God gave him grace to help us in all."

Here's What You Can Do:

Take a statue of Joseph, and bury it upside down, so that it is facing the house. (Don't forget to take Joseph with you if you move.)

And Here's What You Can Say:

Dear Saint Joseph,
Carpenter and father
Builder and protector of homes
Help me with my request

Bonus Ritual!

It is still customary in some parts of Eastern Europe to set a place at the table for Joseph when a family is in special need of his protection, and to invite his statue to dine. Generous servings are doled out to the statue's plate, which are then given to the poor.

Bonus Ritual (II)!

Supplicants can also invoke Saint Joseph for finding a spouse through a Saint Joseph novena. Make sure

you're ready to take yourself off the market; he's ru-
mored to be a powerful ally.

𝒴ou can actually buy prepackaged Saint Joseph
home-selling kits in many religious goods stores.
These modest kits usually provide a plastic statue of
Saint Joseph, some suggested prayers to use when
asking for his help, and guidelines for effectively
invoking him to sell your house. (But you can
save the $7.95 by doing it yourself following our
instructions.)

Saint Joseph has two official Feast Days:
March 19 and May 1.

If you're worried about your dog, cat, bird, fish, iguana, pot-bellied pig . . . or any other type of domestic pet, try calling on Saint Thomas the Apostle.

A good man in a pinch, despite his nickname of "Doubting Thomas," Thomas was also known as Didymus (or "the twin"). He is famous for failing to believe the early reports reaching his ears that Jesus had risen from the dead. He would only be convinced, he said, when he could place his hand in the risen Christ's wounds. This invited Jesus' notable response that defines the essence of faith: "Blessed are those who have not seen and yet believe."

Little is known of the remainder of Thomas's life, although the *Acts of Thomas*, a rather spurious biography, supposedly recounts his missionary efforts in India. Legend says he was martyred finally while preaching in Malabar, on the coast in southern India.

If none of this seems particularly relevant to animal husbandry, it's because there is nothing obvious about the facts of Saint Thomas's life that make such a patronage logical. Rather, it's more likely that because the feast day of Thomas falls near the winter solstice, he has become linked with many practices that should be attributed to pagan gods and spirits. Specifically, in the agricultural communities in which the cult of Thomas flourished most strongly, healthy animals (for breeding, slaughtering, and laboring in the fields) were an economic necessity. He was invoked to ensure their well-being for the coming year.

Here's What You Can Do:

Take a green branch from a tree. Fir, pine, or some sort of evergreen is best. Sprinkle it with water and salt. (Holy water was traditionally used.) Touch each animal in your household while saying the prayer below.

For added measure, place the green bough on your wall and keep it there for a year, and your domestic animals will be blessed with unprecedented vitality.

And Here's What You Can Say:

As you touch each animal with the branch:

Saint Thomas, preserve thee from all sickness.

Bonus Ritual!

For those people who are curious about where they will be living in the next twelve months: On Saint Thomas's Feast Day (either one) throw a shoe backward over your shoulder and go to bed without looking at it. In the morning, if the shoe is pointing toward the door, you will be changing your residence within the year.

There are many other strange beliefs associated with Thomas. In medieval England, where he was invoked against witches, it was said you could hear him riding a horse furiously about in the night before his feast day dawned, fighting evil in the community. It was also simultaneously said to be (a) unlucky to be married on his feast day because, as it was one of the shortest days of the year, it was an omen that the marriage would be short; and (b) lucky to be married on that day because the couple would have "less time left for repentance." Whatever.

Saint Thomas's Feast Day was traditionally December 21, but is now also celebrated on July 3.

Worried about being assaulted? Robbed?

Saint Michael the Archangel

will protect you personally against violence of any kind——and your home against burglary, theft, or vandalism.

Michael, whose name means "like God," doesn't fit the usual saint mold for the simple reason that he wasn't human. Michael never actually lived on earth. He is an archangel—a soldier of heaven, a special messenger from God to humankind. He's listed in the Scriptures as a protector of Israel and, as one of the four archangels who hold up God's throne, "one of the chief princes of heaven." Since the time of the apostles he has been revered as someone with special powers of protection.

In the Book of Revelation, you'll find the story of how Michael and his angels overcame the Devil, making sure he "was cast into the earth and his angels thrown down with him." Michael is often painted wearing heavy armor and carrying a sword, and is referred to by Saint Jude as "the great captain." In the United States, Michael is primarily invoked as the patron saint of police, as well as a heavenly sympathizer for crime victims.

Place a statue of Saint Michael in your house, place of business, or anyplace where you seek protection from theft, intrusion, or trespassers.

And Here's What You Can Say:

Michael the Archangel,

Protect me against all wickedness

Make my home a fortress of peace

A safeguard of love

A wellspring of hope

A haven from violence.

Odd Saint Fact:

In some early British paintings, Michael is depicted hanging out in a cemetery, spookily weighing the worth of newly deceased souls on a special Scale of Justice. No one is quite sure of the origin of this particular aspect of the Michael legend.

Saint Michael the Archangel's Feast Day
is September 29.

Saint Christopher

For Wandering Souls

Travel Insurance for an Increasingly Mobile Planet

Comes over one an absolute necessity
to move. And what is more,
to move in some particular direction.
A double necessity, then:
to get on the move, and to know whither.
—D. H. Lawrence

Much have I travel'd in the
realms of gold,
And many goodly states
and kingdoms seen.
—John Keats

I have been a stranger in a strange land.
—Moses, from the Book of Exodus 2:22

Statistically we are spending more and more time traveling—whether commuting to work or school, or taking planes and trains to distant cities or even countries for work or family matters. If you get anxious, especially in these days of much-publicized disasters by air and road, call upon one of our trusty travel companions. They've been used for centuries, with good effect, by seasoned wanderers around the world.

$\mathcal{S}aint\ \mathcal{C}hristopher$ is no longer officially acknowledged as a saint by the Catholic Church, being one of those purged by the Vatican's 1969 reform movement. Still, despite his lapsed credentials, Christopher remains immensely popular and continues to be renowned for his ability to protect travelers against accidents, misfortune, or death.

The Christopher legend hails from early in the third century, when Christopher, a giant "of fearsome appearance," pledged to find and serve the most powerful king on earth. He attached himself to various royal rulers, but noticed there always seemed to be someone—or something—that each of his masters was fearful of. Finally, after working his way up the regal power chain, he noticed that his current master, the most mighty emperor on earth, always shuddered and crossed himself at any mention of the devil. Naturally, this intrigued Christopher—and he promptly swore allegiance to Satan. But, lo—eventually, he couldn't help seeing that his new master trembled in terror if he saw a crucifix. This convinced Christopher that Christ was the strongest force, either in heaven or on earth, and he promptly converted.

Other versions of the Christopher story have him enduring numerous trials defending his chastity—yes, this happened to guys, too—as well as his newly found Christian faith. Eventually he was martyred by having his head cut off.

So how does this relate to traveling? Just be patient. According to one version of the Christopher legend, while being instructed in his new Christian faith by a holy hermit, Christopher was told to make himself useful in a "humbling occupation." He chose to live in a small hut and help travelers across a nearby difficult-to-ford river. One day a small child appeared and asked to be carried across, but despite Christopher's massive strength (he was a giant, after all) he could barely handle the child's weight. After being carried safely to the other shore, the child revealed that he was in fact Jesus, and that Christopher had "carried the weight of the whole world" upon his shoulders. The Christ Child then instructed Christopher to plant his staff in the ground, and the next day it miraculously sprouted delicious dates that weary travelers could eat.

Here's What You Can Do:

Display a Saint Christopher medal or Holy Card in a prominent (and visible) place in your car. Or carry a Christopher image in your purse, wallet, or pocket if you are traveling by any other means.

Grant me this day a steady hand

and watchful eye

So no harm will come to others

as I pass by

Protect me as I go my way

And lead me safely to my destiny.

Bonus Ritual!

Even if you're not traveling anywhere, a very comforting tradition says that if you look at an image of Saint Christopher before noon, you will be protected against sudden death for the remainder of that day.

Here's the medieval rhyme (updated from Old English) that promises this security:

If thou the face of Christopher on

any morn shall see,

Through the day from sudden

death thou shalt preserved be.

$\mathcal{T}$he name "Christopher" literally means "Christ bearer," and even the most conservative religious supply stores must, by popular demand, carry Saint Christopher medals and other paraphernalia, despite his lack of official standing in the Church.

Saint Christopher's Feast Day is July 25.

If you're about to embark on a trip, and you want a state-sanctified saint (Christopher being too outré for you), consider Saint Bernard of Clairvaux.

Like the breed of faithful dog that shares his name, Bernard has long aided travelers. He's been at it for more than eight hundred years, mostly through the continued popularity of Bernard's own prayer asking Mary for aid, which is called the *Memorare*.

This abbot and Doctor of the Church (the highest academic honor) was born around 1200 to noble and pious parents in Burgundy, France, near the town of Dijon.

Bernard was educated like other young noblemen of his class, but, fearing he wouldn't have the strength to resist the temptations of the world, he decided at a young age to join the very austere Cistercian order. (Even then, Bernard exhibited his peculiarly stubborn—and persuasive—character. He managed to convince several of his brothers and close friends, all of whom originally scoffed at his plans, to enter the monastery with him.)

It turned out that even the very strict Cistercian reg-
imen wasn't enough for Bernard, and so he gathered
a group of thirty supporters—all young noblemen
who had taken vows of poverty and chastity—and
asked to create his own, even more strict, order of
monks. After receiving approval, Bernard founded
what would become the illustrious Abbey of Clairvaux. Despite being offered a bishopship several
times, Bernard chose to travel throughout Europe
preaching. He turned out to be the Church's
strongest recruiter for what turned out to be the dis-
astrous Second Crusade. (The nine Crusades were
exceedingly bloody wars fought between Christians
and Moslems over control of various aspects of the
Holy Land. The Second Crusade was specifically di-
rected against the Turks, who had captured the ancient city of Edessa. The ferocity of the Turkish army,
coupled with in-fighting, duplicity, and jealousy
within the various Christian battalions, doomed this
Crusade, despite Bernard's tireless efforts.)

Bernard's nonstop travels throughout France and
Germany while founding monasteries (the grand total was more than 160), makes him a natural patron
for wanderers, particularly those who travel by foot.
Bernard probably logged thousands of miles on the
failed Second Crusade alone.

No one's quite sure how Bernard's beautiful prayer,
the *Memorare,* became associated with travel, except
for his renowned wanderlust. In content, the *Memorare* is a testament to Bernard's devotion to Mary,
whom he called "The Gateway of Divine Mercy" and
considered the epitome of human perfection.

It's a mouthful, but these words written by Bernard honoring Mary have been used through the centuries by Catholics about to embark on a journey.

Remember, O Gracious Virgin

Mary, that never was it known

That anyone who fled to thy

protection

Implored thy help

Or sought thy intercession was left

unaided.

Inspired by this confidence

We fly unto thee, O virgin of

virgins, our mother

Before thee we stand, sinful and

sorrowful.

O Mother of the Word Incarnate

despise not our petitions

But in your mercy hear and answer

us.

Odd Saint Fact:

In his 1902 book entitled *Curiosities of Popular Customs*, the author, William Walsh, claims to have traced a strange piece of folklore to Bernard: The saint was supposedly visited twice by Mary, once to rouse him from his sickbed to write yet another sermon; the second time to moisten his lips with her breast milk, which gave him much-needed eloquence for an important speech.

Saint Bernard's Feast Day is August 20.

When you're late for that appointment, and you can't find a parking spot... Or if you're waiting for a bus that won't come... Or if your car has broken down and you need help... Yes, there are saints to help you out, even in such minor (but irritating) cases. Our two favorites: Polycarp and Mother Cabrini.

Polycarp, which sounds like the answer to a knock-knock joke, was an early and very influential bishop of Smyrna—today called Izmir—an ancient city on Turkey's west coast. He was a student and follower of the Apostle John. During a backlash against Christians, Polycarp was arrested and ordered to renounce Jesus. Although he was no spring chicken—legend says he spent a full eighty-six years of his life as a Christian, and we know for a fact that he wasn't baptized at birth—Polycarp held out, saying he would never speak a word against "the King who saved me." He was tied to a stake, killed with a sword, and then burned. (What, they needed to be sure?)

Frances Xavier Cabrini has the honor of being the first American saint. The youngest of thirteen children of an Italian farmer, she was turned away from several convents in Italy because of her poor health. Instead, she became a teacher, and a lay worker for the parish of Codogno, after which she founded the Missionary Sisters of the Sacred Heart. Her dream of going to China was shot down by Church authorities, so instead she emigrated to the United States and devoted herself to working with poor Italian immigrant families in New York, many of whom lived in dreadful conditions. She opened other schools and orphanages in New Orleans, Nicaragua, Chicago, and Buenos Aires before dying of malaria in 1917.

Here's What You Can Say:

To find a parking place:

Polycarp,

Find me a spot.

If waiting overlong for a vehicle to come—whether a bus, taxi, tow truck, or a friend willing to give you a lift:

Mother Cabrini,

Send a machini.

Saint Polycarp's Feast Day is February 23; Saint Frances Cabrini's Feast Day is December 22.

Saint Barbara

Miscellaneous Helpers

And Jacks-of-All-Trades in Spiritual Intercession

To everything there is a season, and a
time to every purpose under the heaven:
a time to be born and a time to die;
a time to plant, and a time to pluck up
that which is planted;
a time to kill, and a time to heal;
a time to break down,
and a time to build up;
a time to weep, and a time to laugh;
a time to mourn, and a time to dance;
a time to cast away stones, and a time to
gather stones together;
a time to embrace,
and a time to refrain from embracing;
a time to get, and a time to lose;
a time to keep, and a time to cast away;
a time to rend, and a time to sew;
a time to keep silence,
and a time to speak;
a time to love, and a time to hate;
a time of war, and a time of peace.
—Ecclesiastes 3:1—8

Whatever your worry, or ailment, there's a patron saint to help. Here is a grab bag of those who specialize in a broad range of patronages.

About to have your day in court? Dress nicely, get hold of the best lawyer you can afford —and don't forget to call upon Saint Basil the Great.

Some people are born into families of doctors, lawyers, actors. Basil was born into a family of saints (including, among others, his grandmother, mother, father, sister, and two of his brothers). No surprise that Basil eventually decided to follow them into the family business.

Besides the obvious legacy of piety, Basil's family also had wealth, and so his early life was privileged. In addition to being able to travel to and study in such intellectual and artistic capital cities as Constantinople and Athens, he received a magnificent education. He did finally take his vows, as expected, but not until he was nearly thirty, when he settled into a monastic community near Caesarea, Italy, his hometown.

Basil was known far and wide as an eloquent preacher, especially for his interest in social causes formerly deemed to be secular, such as justice for even the poorest and least respected members of the community.

Basil was a revolutionary in the sense that he believed that monastic life should include the local community as well as society at large, rather than allowing inhabitants to indulge in individual and solitary introspection. It was Basil who encouraged monasteries to welcome guests, found schools and orphanages, and even provide succor for local artists.

After being elected archbishop in A.D. 370, Basil organized soup kitchens, established hospitals, and unceasingly called upon the wealthy to redistribute voluntarily their riches to the less fortunate. A socialist before the term was coined, we see his influence in modern-day activists such as Dorothy Day.

Here's What You Can Do:

Light three candles (red is best) and place next to a picture of Saint Basil.

And Here's What You Can Say:

Saint Basil, friend of the poor

and downtrodden,

Help find me a voice

Protect me from misguided

accusations and unwarranted

punishment

Give me this day peaceful resolve

And I promise to endure with

equanimity.

Saint Basil's Feast Day is January 2. He is also the patron saint of hospital administrators.

Saint Benedict is the holy helper you can turn to when you're the victim of "poison tongues," or gossipmongers.

*B*enedict was born into a wealthy fifth-century Roman family, but decided that the society around him was too full of indulgent and decadent behavior. He gave up his hefty inheritance and headed for the hills. Actually, he went to the mountains, in nearby Subiaco, where he lived as a hermit in a cave for more than three years.

Eventually, Benedict emerged from his cave and began his life's work: founding monasteries. Benedict's Rule—as his famously strict code of practice for monastic life came to be known—went further than even the demanding way preached by the "desert saints" such as Jerome and Antony, who left their homes and families to roam the wastes of northern Egypt in search of perfect solitude.

According to legend, Benedict was often the target of jealousy and intrigue from his fellow monks, many of whom didn't like his admittedly strict rules. There was at least one serious attempt to poison him, but Benedict miraculously survived (which is why he's also the patron saint to evoke on those rare occasions when you believe someone is trying to poison you).

Here's What You Can Say:

Give me the wisdom to discover

The intelligence to understand

The diligence to seek

The patience to wait

The eyes to behold

The heart to meditate

And a life to use proclaiming

the truth.

Bonus Ritual!

Saint Benedict can also be invoked if you've eaten or drunk something that doesn't seem to agree with you. Close your eyes, and make a silent petition to Benedict.

$\mathcal{B}$enedict is also the patron saint of spelunkers (that's cave diving, in plain English) and can also be invoked against witches, in case that's one of your worries.

Saint Benedict's Feast Day is July 11.

If you are desperate, here's a saint for you: **Jude.** *He's the patron saint of last re-sort—the one to turn to for seemingly lost or hopeless cases.*

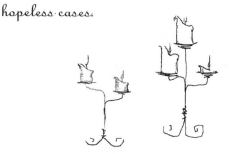

Open up any newspaper to the classified ad section and you'll see dozens of petitions to Saint Jude printed there—along with thanks for those cases in which he has already successfully interceded. (Tradition says he should be both petitioned and thanked in a public way.)

Jude, also known as Thaddeus, was born in a tiny village in Galilee. His father was the brother of Saint Joseph, Jesus' father; his mother was a cousin of Mary, Jesus' mother. Jude lived down the street from Jesus, and he and his brother James were youthful playmates of Jesus. Both Jude and James were destined to become apostles. Not to be confused with Judas, the traitor, Jude was greatly beloved. He has often been called "the most optimistic saint" because he brings hope whenever he is invoked, and he led a long, holy, and productive life serving Christ. Jude was killed while preaching in Persia with Saint Simon.

So how did Jude become associated with hopeless causes? The most reliable explanation is that early Christians confused poor Jude with the disreputable Judas Iscariot, Jesus' betrayer. As a result, no one ever prayed to Jude. Subsequently the unfairly shunned Jude became doubly eager—and worked doubly hard—to help anyone who came to him.

Numerous charitable and beneficent societies devoted to Saint Jude thrive throughout the world. In Chicago, the Saint Jude League includes the entire Chicago police department as members. (The association is pledged to pray and offer help to any member's friend or family who is in a desperate situation. It also does significant charitable work.) Membership in this and other Jude groups is not limited to Catholics, or even Christians. Anyone wishing to help others in dire circumstances is invited to join.

Here's What You Can Do:

Petition Saint Jude by writing out your wish or hopeless cause. Place the paper in a prominent place—on your refrigerator, on your bathroom mirror, on the dashboard of your car. Every morning for nine days speak your request aloud, accompanied by the following prayer:

And Here's What You Can Say:

Dear Saint Jude,
Please help me with my desperate
situation (*name it*),

I need hope and confidence
That my situation can get better
Please use your infinite wisdom
and mercy
To intercede on my behalf.

Saint Jude's Feast Day is June 29.

Don't assume that Saint Nicholas is synonymous with Santa Claus—although that's certainly one of his most popular guises. The real Saint Nicholas is much more complex, and the kind of help he can provide to petitioners is much more versatile. Most commonly, Nicholas is patron of children—and not just because he disperses toys at Christmas when wearing his red Santa costume. Tradition says he saved three young women from lives on the street by throwing bags of gold through their windows at night.

The cult of Saint Nicholas is one of the strongest and most enduring through Eastern Europe. Yet, as with so many early saints, the actual facts of his life remain obscure, and the legends surrounding him tell of a darker and more ambivalent spirit than what we've come to popularly associate with the name in Western culture.

What *is* known about the real Nicholas is simply this: He was born in the fourth century in the town of Lycia, which today would be located in southwestern Turkey. He entered the Church at a young age, and eventually was appointed bishop of Myra.

The legends surrounding Nicholas are much more colorful. One Nicholas story—scholars say it's a dubious one—says he restored three boys to life after they were drowned in a brine tub by an evil butcher. Another asserts that he generously gave three bags of gold to three young girls—Christian virgins all—in order to save them from prostitution (they used the gold as dowries to attract respectable Christian husbands). Yet another story tells how he miraculously rescued three sailors from a violent storm off the coast of what is now known as Turkey.

So how did Nicholas eventually become best known as the benevolent Santa Claus? It seems that the stories of Nicholas's generosity, especially toward children, became confused with various northern European folk stories about a pagan "gift giver" with tremendous magical powers, and who periodically appeared in order to reward the good—and, perhaps more significantly—punish the wicked.

Many of our current Christmas customs have their origins in pagan times, when the New Year was a time of much ritualistic superstition to ensure good luck in the coming year. (Indeed, early Christian leaders forbade any Christmas celebrations at all, assuming quite correctly that they had more to do with pagan tradition than with celebration of the birth of Jesus.)

Interestingly, the so-called gift giver found in so many different cultures' lore could as easily have a female form as a male one. And he (or she) was accompanied on his rounds by strange and frightening nonhuman creatures whose job was to inflict painful and humiliating punishment on anyone who had sinned.

Here's What You Can Do:

Put out hay and sugar for Saint Nicholas's horses before you go to bed at night.

And Here's What You Can Say:

Dear Saint Nicholas, please grant

me my request.

Bless and protect the children of

this house.

Bonus Ritual!

One odd custom that still can be found in some rural British schools involves children barring the teacher from school on Shrove Tuesday, Saint Nicholas's feast day, while chanting:

Pardon, master, pardon
Pardon in a pin;
If you don't give us a holiday
We won't let you in.

Odd Saint Fact:

Women who had been unfaithful to their husbands apparently had the most to fear during Saint Nicholas's visitations. On his official feast day, local buffoons would dress up in odd costumes and publicly torment women thought to have sinned in that particular way.

Saint Nicholas's Feast Day is December 6.

$\mathcal{S}$aint $\mathcal{B}$arbara, as befits her fiery and stubborn temperament, is invoked against thunderstorms, lightning, and fire.

$\mathcal{B}$arbara was a beautiful fourth-century Syrian princess who converted to Christianity against the will of her pagan father. Unlike most other saints of this category (who are invariably female and collectively known as "the virgin martyrs"), Barbara was not married off to a lusty pagan nobleman or sent off to be debauched in a brothel. Instead, she was locked away in a remote stone tower by her controlling father, who was apparently equally enraged by her deep religious faith and her irresistible sex appeal. (For good measure, he dug a deep moat around the tower to discourage any visitors.)

Yet word of Barbara's goodness, beauty, and virtue spread far and wide, and she became so famous as a miraculous healer that crowds camped around the tower, hoping to get a glimpse of, or be blessed by her. Barbara's malevolent father, angered at the ingenious attempts she made to sanctify her dreary tower in the name of Christ, tried doing away with her in a number of creative ways. He succeeded eventually—but not before getting *his* just deserts.

One day, while her intolerable parent was out of town on business, Barbara asked a local workman to cut a third window in the tower. (It had two windows, but Barbara wanted another one as a way of paying homage to the Holy Trinity.) After the window was created, Barbara made the sign of the cross beside it to express her gratitude. Miraculously, the stone softened and she was able to carve the Christian cross into the wall. When her father returned, he was naturally furious—and swore he would kill his daughter for these latest outrages. But as he leaped at her, Barbara grew wings, flew out her new window, and escaped. Unfortunately, her taste of freedom was brief. She lived as a hermit in the mountains, devoting herself to prayer and meditation, for only a short time before being betrayed by an untrustworthy shepherd. Her father beheaded Barbara in a gruesome public ceremony—but at the instant of her martyrdom, a huge thunderstorm descended upon the town and her odious father was struck down by a lightning bolt. (It's therefore somewhat ironic that Barbara is called upon to protect people from thunderstorms and lightning, but this is perhaps evidence of her true Christian charity.)

Here's What You Can Do:

𝒫lace a sweet treat (such as a piece of cake, a cookie, or some candy) on a plate along with a drop of honey and a piece of wheat (yes, some sort of whole-grain cereal is fine). Sprinkle the offering with perfume. Rosewater is best, but any sweet, light scent will do the trick.

Light a candle (again, a rose-scented or red-colored one is ideal).

Dear Saint Barbara,

Intercede for me

Protect me from this storm

With your mighty strength

Make my fear go away

And peace return.

Bonus Ritual!

One interesting but seemingly random ritual associated with Saint Barbara has long been performed by European girls hoping to get married. They place a branch from a cherry or peach tree in water; if the branch flowers within the month, they know they are sure to wed within the year.

Saint Barbara's Feast Day is December 4.

$\mathcal{S}$aint $\mathcal{S}$within is known as "the watery saint" throughout Great Britain. You can ask for his versatile and obliging talent for bringing, preventing, or stopping rain.

Saint Swithin (also spelled Swithun) was the childhood tutor of a fourteenth-century British king, Ethelwulth, and later became one of his most valued counselors. After being made bishop of Winchester, Swithin became famous for his charitable gifts to the poor—and for his kindness and personal humility.

Despite having long held the powerful post of bishop of Winchester—a highly influential position within the political and religious hierarchy of medieval England—Swithin's dying wish was to be buried outside the church, so that "the rain could fall on me, as on all of God's creatures." (The traditional residing spot for a bishop would be in a grand—and prominently displayed—crypt within the cathedral.)

When, a few centuries after Swithin's death, an attempt was made to move his remains to its "proper" place inside the church, a violent storm broke out. It rained for nearly forty days (catch the symbolism?), causing havoc in the local agricultural economy.

Most aspects of the Swithin legend revolve around rain, and a number of surviving medieval rhymes testify to superstitions attached to this kindly saint.

If on Saint Swithin's it does rain
For forty days it will remain
If Swithin's day be fair and clear
It betides a happy year
If Swithin's day be dark with rain
Then will be dear all sorts of grain.

$\mathcal{P}$lace a statue (or picture) of Saint Swithin on your windowsill so he faces the outdoors. Tell him your desire: more rain? less? a little snow? Whatever. Just say the word.

And Here's What You Can Say:

Saint Swithin,
Hear our request
Give us the perfect quantity of
water for our needs.

Bonus Ritual!

$\mathcal{I}$n addition to his reputation as a powerful "weather saint"—yes, this is a category of patron sainthood— Swithin can also be used as a healer. Medieval pilgrims would make the journey to his grave in Winchester to request help with specific health issues; Saint Swithin's reputation for kindness and charity is so great, you can probably ask him to intercede on your behalf even if you can't afford the time or the money to travel to England.

Odd Saint Fact:

$\mathcal{I}$t has long been considered unlucky to get married on Saint Swithin's Day. So plan your wedding date carefully.

Saint Swithin's Feast Day is July 15.

$\mathcal{S}$aint $\mathcal{L}$awrence offers a good way to remind yourself to keep a sense of humor when things aren't going particularly well in the kitchen.

$\mathcal{L}$awrence was a devout Roman priest who had been elected one of Rome's "seven deacons" and made responsible for the Church's charitable work among the local poor.

When the reigning pope of Lawrence's day, Saint Sixtus, was condemned to death in 258 by local pagan authorities, the loyal and affectionate Lawrence was utterly bereft—until he was reassured by Saint Sixtus's prediction that Lawrence would be following him (that is, dying) within three days. This cheered Saint Lawrence up no end, and he went on a philanthropic spree, giving away all the Church's riches to the poor and needy. A few days later, when government officials decreed that the vast wealth of the Church be handed over to the emperor, Lawrence went through town and gathered up all the cripples and misfits and beggars. These he took to the emperor, saying, "Here are the Church's treasures." He was promptly sentenced to death for his wit.

And here's the reason that Saint Lawrence has become the patron of cooks and restaurateurs. Furious at Lawrence's insubordination, the emperor had him tied to an iron grill and roasted slowly over a hot fire. Rather than showing any sign of discomfort, Lawrence was so pleased that he would soon be joining his God that he prayed aloud joyfully even as his flesh cooked. At one point, he cheerfully turned to his torturers and said, "Turn me over, I'm done on this side."

Here's What You Can Do:

$\mathcal{L}$ight two candles in your kitchen, taking care to place one on a higher surface than the other (for example, one on the counter and one on the floor). Allow them to burn for at least fifteen minutes, then switch their positions.

Patience, humor, joy
Lawrence, help me achieve these all.

Bonus Ritual!

We know devout Catholics who like to quote Saint Lawrence's final words when they are suffering from heat—in the dog days of summer, for instance. "Saint Lawrence, I'm done on this side" is a gentle reminder to God that the temperature is becoming a bit too . . . intense.

Odd Saint Fact:

Lawrence was also known in Rome as Il Cortese Spagnuolo, "the Courteous Spaniard." This is because two hundred years after his death, his sarcophagus was opened to receive the relics of Saint Stephen, and the bones of Saint Lawrence considerately moved over to give the place of honor to his fellow saint.

Apparently, the gridiron on which he was grilled was preserved in the Church of San Lorenzo in Rome; and two churches in that city preserve portions of his melted fat. (Hey, we never said martyrdom was pretty.) Lawrence's ribs, arms, and shoulder blades are scattered among many churches throughout Europe.

Saint Lawrence (Feast Day: August 10) is also the patron saint of cutlers, glaziers, and the poor.

Call Saint Cecilia the "it" girl of the third century. Possessing an endearingly quirky style, Cecilia can be called upon by musicians and other performers suffering from pre-performance anxiety.

Cecilia was a beautiful young Christian virgin (that phrase is becoming awfully familiar, no?) betrothed against her will to a well-meaning young man called Valerian, who was unfortunately (for Cecilia) a pagan. Immediately following the wedding ceremony, Cecilia dressed herself in sackcloth, covered herself with ashes, and begged Valerian not to force her to consummate the marriage, as she had vowed to give her virginity to God. She then whispered to her new husband that if he tried to force her, he would regret it, as an angel stood guard over her. Valerian's gentle response to this strange confidence was merely to ask, "My dearest one, if this is true, where is the angel?"

When Cecilia promised him he could see the angel for himself if he converted to Christianity, Valerian promptly trotted off to the Pope to be baptized. After returning a proper Christian, he was miraculously able to see Cecilia's guardian angel, and fell to his knees in wonder. The angel was in the process of placing elaborate crowns woven of fresh roses and lilies on the heads of the newlyweds when Valerian's brother wandered into the room. (It seems to have been an informal household.) The brother was so impressed by the sight and scent of flowers out of season—he couldn't see the angel, still being pagan himself—that *he* immediately converted. The two brothers and Cecilia subsequently went on to do much good Christian missionary work before being—you guessed it—condemned to die for their faith. All three are honored as martyrs.

Cecilia is called upon by musicians and music lovers because of a mystical vision she experienced during her wedding. As the pagan ceremony neared completion Cecilia heard a wonderful choir of angels singing, and the following words came to her mind as if spoken aloud: "May my heart remain unsullied so that I am not confounded." Cecilia is frequently painted with an organ or other musical instrument that indicates her patronage.

$\mathscr{F}$ind a quiet room (or quiet corner backstage) before your performance. Hum or recite part of the piece you will be performing, then say the following prayer:

And Here's What You Can Say:

Dear Saint Cecilia, who stood

strong in the face of terror,

Intercede so that my heart

remains pure

And I remain unconfounded

by fear.

Saint Cecilia's Feast Day is November 22.

Saint Andrew has a number of interesting rituals associated with him, very few of which seem to have to do with his "official" patronage of fishermen. He is most frequently appealed to by people who are having trouble choosing a profession.

Andrew himself was originally a fisherman who left his profession to follow Christ. Already a disciple of John the Baptist, Andrew was helping John in his early attempts to convince people that the true Messiah was soon to come. It is to Andrew that John the Baptist famously said, "Behold the Lamb of God!" when Jesus came to the River Jordan to be baptized, in recognition that the Messiah had indeed finally arrived.

Andrew was the first of the twelve apostles to join Jesus. He later convinced his brother, Peter, to join them. In fact, Andrew and Peter are the recipients of Jesus' notable invitation to drop their fishing vocations to become "fishers of men." One theory says

Andrew's midlife career change is the reason he has become associated with career counseling.

After Jesus' death, Andrew traveled to Greece and Turkey, where he supposedly established the Church in Constantinople (now Istanbul). Andrew, like Jesus, was put to death on a cross, but he was tied to it, not nailed, as was in fact the more traditional way of that time. During the three days it took Andrew to slowly die, he courageously continued preaching, and converted many of the pagans who had come to mock him.

As Andrew was hung from his cross—and subsequently died—in an off-kilter manner, a "Saint Andrew's cross," as it has come to be called, is shaped like an "X." Saint Andrew's cross forms the background of the British flag (and is overlaid with the cross of Saint George).

Here's What You Can Do:

$\mathcal{M}$elt a piece of wax on a spoon (or other appropriate utensil) and drop into a bowl filled with cold water. The shape of the cooled wax will reveal your true profession. For example, a musical instrument indicates you will be a musician; a pen, that you will be a writer; a weapon, that you are destined to be a soldier.

Odd Saint Fact:

$\mathcal{B}$ecause he is the patron saint of Scotland, Saint Andrew's feast day has become the excuse for all sorts of nonspiritual and nonfishermanlike behavior. November 30 has become a patriotic holiday for the Scots, providing a wonderful opportunity to go squirrel hunting (squirrel and haggis are traditional dishes on Saint Andrew's Day) and to drink great quantities of alcohol. The link between Andrew and Scotland is at best tenuous, but one legend says that Saint Regulus was visited by an angel who instructed him to collect Andrew's remains, get in a boat, and build a shrine wherever the winds and tides of the ocean might take him. That turned out to be Fife, Scotland; today you can still visit the shrine of Saint Andrew, where his mortal remains supposedly rest.

Saint Andrew (Feast Day: November 30) is also the patron saint of Russia and Greece.

$\mathcal{S}$aint $\mathcal{F}$rancis of $\mathcal{A}$ssisi is the saint we all love to love, who somehow managed, despite the many wrong turns he took in life, to win affection from everyone who knew him. $\mathcal{A}$s the patron of ecologists and nature lovers, $\mathcal{F}$rancis is who you turn to when you are dismayed about damage or injury to the natural world.

Saint Francis was born the son of a wealthy cloth merchant in late twelfth-century Assisi. His father groomed him from an early age to take over the family business, and indeed young Francis turned out to be a savvy businessman—and quite the party boy. His biographer wrote that Francis was "addicted to evil" in his youth; yet, despite his getting into trouble time and time again, Francis's enormous charm always got him back in the good graces of his family, and society.

Eventually, Francis's business dealings took him to France, where he made his father enough money to keep him very happy—and where Francis indulged in enough partying to satisfy even his apparently rowdy tastes. Yet he grew tired of what was an almost purely hedonistic lifestyle, and turned his attention toward worldly conquests of another kind: He decided to join the Crusades, not for reasons of faith or religious conviction, but simply to win fame and glory as a soldier.

But here is where God finally intervened. As Francis was riding toward battle he had a vision that instructed him in no uncertain terms to abandon any thoughts of war, and to return to Assisi, where another role awaited him. Francis obeyed, headed home—and was in for a rude awakening. For the first time in his life the golden boy found himself out of favor. The formerly adoring townspeople mocked him for a coward; his father was furious that Francis had brought shame upon the family name. Francis retired to a cave to pray and meditate, but for some months was deeply torn between carrying on his successful commercial enterprises (despite their falling out, he continued to work for his father) and devoting himself to God. One day, when riding aimlessly around the countryside, Francis went into a small church in the rustic Italian town of San Damiano. To his astonishment, he heard a voice, coming from a crucifix above the altar, that said: "Repair my falling house."

Francis promptly rode back home, helped himself to some bolts of costly material from his father's clothing business, and sold it to get enough cash to obey the voice's instructions. Caught before he was able to carry out any action, Francis was dragged into court by his father. Francis promptly returned the money, then proceeded to strip himself naked in front of the entire community. He told the crowd that naturally gathered that he no longer considered he had an earthly father, and that "now I can truly say, Our Father, who art in heaven."

Francis went on to become a great preacher and the founder of the Franciscan order, which emphasizes charity to the poor as well as obedience to the Church. There are numerous wonderful stories about Francis, and his quirky but always generous reaction to the fallible human world around him. Once a priest was dragged in front of him for living openly with a woman. Francis's reaction was to kneel before the priest and kiss his hands—because the hands had held the host during Mass, which meant they had held God.

The most famous Francis story is how he preached to the birds, telling them they should be thankful to God for their clothes, their freedom, and for God's constant care of them. The birds stood absolutely still as he spoke. Francis was a popular Renaissance painting subject; artists frequently depicted him surrounded by tame beasts, a representation of an ideal state of natural innocence.

The enormous charm and magnetism that Francis had as a young man stayed with him. He was said to be able to read the Gospel with such emotion and devotion that anyone who listened would weep. He reportedly suffered from the stigmata, a painful but blessed condition in which a holy man or woman physically manifests the same wounds Christ suffered on the cross.

Plant a flower, provide food to a wild animal, or simply sit in the middle of nature. Do this for nine days in a row while saying Saint Francis's famous prayer:

And Here's What You Can Say:

Lord, make me an

instrument of your peace

Where there is hatred,

let me sow love

Where there is injury, pardon

Where there is doubt, faith

Where there is despair, hope

Where there is darkness, light

And where there is sadness, joy.

Saint Francis of Assisi's Feast Day is October 4.

$\mathcal{S}aint\ \mathcal{E}xpeditus$ is heaven's certified financial planner. A good man to know in a pinch.

Saint Expeditus is another one of those saints who may simply have been the figment of an overly active imagination. We love him not despite, but because of, his colorful and doubtful origins. The Expeditus legend—aprocryphal most certainly, mean-spirited possibly—says this saint was an anonymous Armenian martyred saint whose remains were shipped from Rome to a convent in Paris for burial. These bones were in a box labeled *spedito*—Italian for special delivery. The Parisian nuns, they say, assumed the Latin translation of *spedito*, or Expeditus, to be the name of the saint. Or perhaps they were just showing disdain for the secular language of their southern neighbors. Whatever the truth, a new saint was born.

Expeditus became, not surprisingly, the patron saint of procrastination. But for some unknown reason, this history-impaired saint is also invoked by people who need money. The only connection we can see is that procrastinators are also those who often fall short in money matters—somehow, the checks don't get out on time, the work doesn't get done, the loan isn't repaid promptly. (Send a Saint Expeditus prayer card to the procrastinator who owes you, and see if it helps.)

Here's What You Can Say:

For a specific money problem:

Saint Expeditus,
help me obtain enough
financial resources
so I can live
peacefully and contentedly.
Let my heart be full,
my needs few.

For long-term good luck with money:

Saint Expeditus,
I trust in your help
to obtain everything
I truly need.

Place a picture of Saint Expeditus on a windowsill (yes, it is possible to find pictures representing him. If you can't get your hands on one, it's perfectly acceptable to draw your own). Then, place some coins in a cup next to the picture. Say one of the preceding prayers. After your request has been granted, you may take most of the coins out of the cup, but always leave at least one to express your gratitude. You should also thank Saint Expeditus by giving alms (money, food, or clothes) to a child, an elderly person, or a pregnant woman. (We happen to think this is a good idea in any case.)

Saint Expeditus (Feast Day: April 19) is also the patron saint of emergencies and solutions.

Prayers

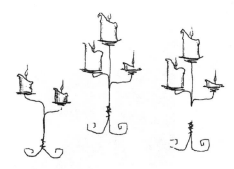

The Doxology (Glory Be)

Glory be to the Father, and to the Son, and to the Holy Spirit.

As it was in the beginning, is now, and ever shall be, world without end.

Amen.

Gloria Patri, et Filio, et Spiritui Sancto. Sicut erat in principio, et nunc,

et semper, et in saecula saeculorum.

Amen.

The Memorare

Remember, O most gracious Virgin Mary, that never was it known that anyone who fled to thy protection, implored thy help, or sought thy intercession, was left unaided.

Inspired with this confidence, I fly unto thee, O Virgin of virgins my Mother; to thee do I come, before thee I stand, sinful and sorrowful; O Mother of the Word Incarnate, despise not my petitions, but in thy clemency hear and answer me. Amen.

The Apostles Creed

I believe in God the Father Almighty, Creator of heaven and earth. I believe in Jesus Christ, His only Son, our Lord. He was conceived by the power of the Holy Spirit and born of the Virgin Mary. He suffered under Pontius Pilate, was crucified, died, and was buried. He descended into hell. On the third day He rose again. He ascended into Heaven and is seated at the right hand of the Father. He will come again to judge the living and the dead. I believe in the Holy Spirit, the Holy Catholic Church, the communion of saints, the forgiveness of sins, the resurrection of the body, and the life everlasting. Amen.

The Lord's Prayer (Our Father)

Our Father, who art in heaven, hallowed be thy name; thy kingdom come; thy will be done, on earth as it is in heaven. Give us this day our daily bread; and forgive us our trespasses as we forgive those who trespass against us; and lead us not into temptation, but deliver us from evil. Amen.

The Sign of the Cross

In the name of the Father, and of the Son, and of the Holy Spirit. Amen.

In nomine Patris et Filii, et Spiritus Sancti. Amen.

The Hail Mary

Hail Mary, full of grace. The Lord is with thee. Blessed art thou amongst women, and blessed is the fruit of thy womb, Jesus. Holy Mary, Mother of God, pray for us sinners, now and at the hour of our death. Amen.

Confiteor (I Confess)

I confess to Almighty God, and to you my brothers and sisters, that I have sinned through my own fault; in my thoughts and in my words, in what I have done, and in what I have failed to do; and I ask blessed Mary, ever Virgin, and all the angels and saints, and you, my brothers and sisters, to pray for me to the Lord our God. Amen.

Novena

A novena is nine days of prayer, either public or private, dedicated to a particular saint or member of the Holy Trinity (God the Father, God the Son, or God the Holy Spirit). There are no set prayers for a novena; an individual may perform a private novena, or an organized novena can be performed at a given time and place. Most novenas contain an "indulgence," or a request that a particular sin be forgiven, and often, novenas are said in order to petition a saint for a specific request. (For example, many novenas are said for the sake of the souls in Purgatory.) Many Catholic churches sponsor novenas for a particular saint, attended by both local parishioners and pilgrims who have traveled to the church specifically for this purpose. Novenas are traditionally held on the nine days preceding that saint's feast day. Private novenas can be held anytime, and are most commonly performed in honor of the Virgin Mary, Saint Jude, Saint Anne, Saint Antony, or Saint Joseph; there are public novenas held around the world before the feasts of Pentecost, the Assumption, and the Immaculate Conception. Like so many modern Catholic rituals, the practice of devoting nine days to honoring a supernatural figure who has the power to intercede in earthly or spiritual matters originated in pagan Roman times, but was entrenched in the Christian world by the seventeenth century.

The Rosary

The Rosary is a spiritual "bouquet of roses" that Catholics offer to Mary, the mother of Jesus, in the form of a set series of prayers.

You may have seen the necklacelike circle of beads that some Catholics use when praying. This is the physical representation of the Rosary, and it helps the person praying keep track of—and concentrate on—the prayers being said.

Every set of Rosary beads contains a crucifix followed by sequences of large beads, small beads, and "spaces" of chain that separate the groups of beads. The prayers associated with the physical aspect of the Rosary are as follows:

At the crucifix: Say one Apostles Creed (there is only one crucifix on any set of beads).

For every large bead: Say one Our Father.

For every small bead: Say one Hail Mary.

For every space in the chain between sets of beads: Say one Glory Be.

After the opening sequence of prayers (one Apostles Creed, one Our Father, three Hail Marys, One Glory Be) the beads are grouped into "decades" that include one Our Father, ten Hail Marys and one Glory Be. A complete Rosary contains fifteen decades, each of which represents a "Mystery" in the life of Jesus. There are five "Joyful Mysteries," five "Sorrowful Mysteries," and five "Glorious Mysteries" as follows:

Joyful Mysteries

—The Annunciation
—The Visitation
—The Nativity
—The Presentation
—Finding in the Temple

Sorrowful Mysteries

—Agony in the Garden
—Scourging at the Pillar
—Crowning of Thorns
—Carrying of the Cross
—The Crucifixion

The Glorious Mysteries

—The Resurrection
—The Ascension
—The Descent of the Holy Spirit
—The Assumption
—The Coronation of Mary

The person praying should meditate on a specific Mystery as he or she says the prayers in the Rosary.

It is traditional to vary the Mystery with the day of the week, as follows:

Monday: Joyful Mysteries
Tuesday: Sorrowful Mysteries
Wednesday: Glorious Mysteries
Thursday: Joyful Mysteries
Friday: Sorrowful Mysteries
Saturday: Glorious Mysteries
Sundays in Advent and up until Lent: Joyful Mysteries
Sundays during Lent: Sorrowful Mysteries
All other Sundays: Glorious Mysteries

It is also traditional to have a new set of Rosary beads blessed by a priest. Each bead in a set of blessed Rosary beads will give its owner an "indulgence," or fogiveness, for a sin that would otherwise need to be suffered for in purgatory.

Index of Patronages
Assigned to Saints

A

Accountants
Matthew

Actors
Genesius

Air travelers
Joseph of Cupertino

Animals
Francis of Assisi

Architects
Barbara, Thomas

Art
Catherine of Bologna

Artists
Luke

Athletes
Sebastian

Authors
Francis de Sales

Aviators
Thérèse of Lisieux,
Joseph of Cupertino

B

Bakers
Elizabeth of Hungary,
Nicholas

Bankers
Matthew

Barren women
Anne

Blind
Raphael the Archangel,
Lucy

Booksellers
John of God

Boy Scouts
George

Brewers
Augustine of Hippo,
Luke,
Nicholas of Myra

Bricklayers
Stephen

Brides
Nicholas of Myra

Broadcasters
Gabriel the Archangel

Builders
Vincent Ferrer, Barbara

Businesswomen
Margaret of Clitherow

C

Cab drivers
Fiacre

Cancer victims
Peregrine Laziosi

Carpenters
Joseph

Childbirth
Gerard Majella

Children
    Nicholas of Myra
Civil servants
    Thomas More
Comedians
    Vitus
Cooks
    Lawrence

D
Dairy workers
    Brigid
Dancers
    Vitus
Deaf
    Francis de Sales
Dentists
    Apollonia
Desperate situations
    Jude, Rita of Cascia
Disabled
    Giles
Doctors
    Luke
Domestic animals
    Antony
Domestic workers
    Zita
Dying
    Joseph

E
Ecologists
    Francis of Assisi
Editors
    John Bosco

Emigrants
    Frances Xavier Cabrini
Engineers
    Patrick
Epidemics
    Godeberta
Epilepsy
    Vitus
Eye disease
    Clare, Lucy
Expectant mothers
    Gerard

F
Falsely accused
    Raymund Nonnatus
Farmers
    Isidore the Farmer
Fathers
    Joseph
Fire fighters
    Florian
Fire prevention
    Catherine of Siena,
    Agatha
Fishermen
    Andrew, Peter
Florists
    Thérèse of Lisieux

G
Gardeners
    Fiacre
Girls
    Agnes, Ursula
Grocers
    Michael

H

Hairdressers
  Martin de Porres
Headaches
  Teresa of Avila
Hospitals
  John of God
Housewives
  Anne
Hotelkeepers
  Amand

I

Immigrants
  Frances Xavier Cabrini
Impossible cases
  Rita of Cascia, Jude
Invalids
  Roch

J

Journalists
  Francis de Sales
Judges/Jurists
  John of Capistrano

L

Laborers
  James, Joseph
Lawyers
  Thomas More
Learning
  Ambrose
Lost or desperate causes
  Jude, Rita of Cascia
Lost articles
  Antony of Padua

Lovers
  Valentine

M

Maids
  Zita
Married women
  Anne, Monica
Mentally ill
  Dymphna, Christina the
  Astonishing
Merchants
  Francis of Assisi,
  Nicholas of Myra
Messengers
  Gabriel the Archangel
Mothers
  Monica, Anne
Musicians
  Cecelia, Gregory

N

Neurological disorders
  Dymphna
Nurses
  Agatha, John of God

P

Painters
  Luke
Pestilence (relief)
  Roch (Rocco)
Philosophers
  Catherine of Alexandria
Physicians
  Luke

Poets
    David, Columba
Poison sufferers
    Benedict
Police officers
    Michael
Poor
    Antony of Padua,
    Lawrence
Postal workers
    Gabriel the Archangel
Preachers
    Catherine of Alexandria,
    John Chrysostom
Pregnant women
    Gerard Majella
Priests
    John Vianney
Printers
    Augustine, Genesius,
    John of God
Prisoners
    Dismas
Public relations
    Bernadine of Siena

R
Radio workers
    Gabriel the Archangel
Rheumatoid sufferers
    James the Greater

S
Sailors
    Erasmus (Elmo)
Schools
    Thomas Aquinas

Scientists
    Albert the Great
Sculptors
    Claude
Secretaries
    Genesius
Servants
    Martha, Zita
Sick
    John of God
Skiers
    Bernard
Snakebite victims
    Hilary
Social justice
    Joseph
Social workers
    Louise de Marillac
Soldiers
    George, Martin of Tours
Speakers (Orators)
    John Chrysostom
Stomach disorders
    Elmo, Timothy
Stone masons
    Stephen
Students
    Catherine of Alexandria,
    Thomas Aquinas
Surgeons
    Luke

T
Tax collectors
    Matthew
Taxi drivers
    Fiacre

Teachers
    Gregory the Great,
    John Baptist de la Salle
Television
    Clare of Assisi
Throat ailments
    Blaise
Travelers
    Raphael the Archangel,
    Nicholas of Myra,
    Antony of Padua,
    Christopher

V

Vintners
    Amand, Morand
Vocations
    Andrew, Alphonsus

W

Women giving birth
    Margaret, Gerard, Anne
Writers
    Francis de Sales

CLARE LA PLANTE is an Evanston, Illinois-based writer and teacher who makes frequent appeals to Saint Antony and Saint Rita for both the things she has lost and the things she hopes to find. Her big sister ALICE writes, teaches, and worries in Palo Alto, California, where she finds herself constantly entreating Saint Jude for emergency aid with her various impossible situations.

A Select Bibliography

Attwater, Donald, ed. *The Penguin Dictionary of Saints*. New York: Penguin, 1965.

Ball, Ann. *Catholic Traditions in the Garden*. Huntington, Indiana: Our Sunday Visitor Inc., 1998.

Bogle, Joanna. *A Book of Feasts and Seasons*. Leominster, Herefordshire, England: Fowler Wright Books, 1996.

Dues, Greg. *Catholic Customs and Traditions*. Mystic, Connecticut: Twenty-Third Publications, 1993.

Dunn-Mascetti, Manuela. *Saints: The Chosen Few*. New York: Ballantine Books, 1994.

Elie, Paul, ed. *Tremors of Bliss: Contemporary Writers on the Saints*. New York: Harcourt Brace, 1994.

Ellsberg, Robert. *All Saints: Daily Reflections on Saints, Prophets, and Witnesses for Our Time*. New York: Crossroad Publishing Co., 1997.

Elvins, Mark Turnham. *Old Catholic England*. London: Catholic Truth Society, 1978.

Farmer, David, ed. *The Oxford Dictionary of Saints*. New York: Oxford University Press, 1997.

Freze, Michale. *Patron Saints*. Huntington, Indiana: Our Sunday Visitor, 1992.

Gordon, Anne. *A Book of Saints: True Stories of How They Touch Our Lives*. New York: Bantam Books, 1994.

The HarperCollins Encyclopedia of Catholicism. San Francisco: HarperCollins, 1995.

Hayes, Edward. *A Pilgrim's Almanac*. Leavenworth, Kansas: Forest of Peace Publishing, 1989.

Hodorowics Knab, Sophie. *Polish Customs, Traditions & Folklore.* New York: Hippocrene Books, 1996.

Hole, Christina. *The Encyclopedia of Superstitions.* Oxford, England: Helicon Publishing Ltd., 1948.

Hole, Christina. *Saints in Folklore.* New York: M. Barrows and Company Inc., a division of William Harris & Co., 1965.

Howard, Alexander. *Endless Cavalade—A Diary of British Festivals and Customs.* London: Arthur Baker Ltd., 1964.

Koenig-Bricker Woodeene. *Prayers of the Saints.* San Francisco: HarperCollins, 1996.

Loomis, C. Grant. *White Magic: An Introduction to the Folklore of Christian Legend.* Cambridge, Massachusetts: The Mediaeval Academy of America, 1948.

Meyer, Marvin and Richard Smith. *Ancient Christian Magic: Coptic Text of Ritual Power.* San Francisco: Harper, 1994.

Opie, Iona and Moria Tatem. *A Dictionary of Superstitions.* New York: Oxford University Press, 1989.

Schlesinger, Henry. *Everyday Saints: A Guide to Special Prayers.* New York: Avon Books, 1996.

Thomas, Keith. *Religion and the Decline of Magic.* New York: Penguin Books, 1971.

Thompson. Sue Ellen and Barbara Carlson. *Holidays, Festivals, and Celebrations of the World Dictionary.* Detroit, Michigan: Omnigraphics, Inc., 1994.

Walsh, Michael, ed. *Butler's Lives of the Saints.* San Francisco: Harper, 1991.

Walsh, William. *Curiosities of Popular Customs.* Philadelphia: J. B. Lippincott Company, 1925.

Weiser, Francis X. *Handbook of Christian Feasts and Customs.* New York: Harcourt, Brace & World Inc., 1958.

Zeiller, Jacques. *Christian Beginnings.* New York: Hawthorne Books, 1960.

Index

A

Acacius, Saint, 93n
Adversity, 54–56
Agatha, Saint, 90–91
Agnes. Saint, 16, 23–26
Agnus dei (Lamb of God), 10–11
Andrew, Saint, 183–185
Angels, 5
Anne, Saint, 2, 111–113, 197
Antony, Saint, 93n, 161, 197
Antony of Padua, Saint, 1, 68,
    70–73
Anxiety, coping with, 43–67
    adversity, 54–56
    bad habits, 61–62
    depression, 57, 59–60
    insomnia, 63–65, 67
    performance anxiety, 180, 182
    repentant sinners, 44–45
    stress, 46, 47, 49, 52–53
Apollonia, Saint, 95–96
Apostles Creed, 195
Arthritis, 87–89
Augustine, Saint, 40, 41, 61–62,
    101

B

Bachelard, Gaston, 123
Bad habits, 61–62
Barbara, Saint, 93n, 156, 171–173
Barr, Amelia, 17
Basil the Great, Saint, 159–160
Benedict, Saint, 161–163
Benedict's Rule, 161
Bernard of Clairvaux, Saint,
    150–153
Bierce, Ambrose, 77
Blaise, Saint, 93n, 107–110
Book of Ecclesiastes, 157
Book of Exodus, 145
Breasts, diseases of, 90–91
Brigid, Saint, 114–117

C

Cabrini, Saint Frances Xavier, 155
Catherine of Alexandria, Saint,
    19–22, 93n
Cecilia, Saint, 180–182
Cervantes, Miguel de, 123
Charles VII, King of France, 55
Charms, 10–11
Chest pains, 100, 103
Childbirth, 111–113
Christianity, early, 9–10
Christmas traditions, 11, 169
Christopher, Saint, 1, 5, 28, 93n,
    144, 146–149
Confessions (Augustine), 61
Confiteor (I Confess), 197
Congregation for the Causes of
    Saints, 5, 14
Court appearance, 159, 160
Crusades, 151, 187
Curiosities of Popular Customs
    (Walsh), 152
Cyricus, Saint, 93n

D

Dark Night of the Soul, The (John
    of the Cross), 66
Denis, Saint, 93n, 97–99
Depression, 57, 59–60
Dionysius, Saint, 95, 97
Domestic pets, 131, 133–134, 139,
    140
Doxology, The (Glory Be), 194

E

Edward III, King of England, 125
Eliot, T.S., 47
Elmo, Saint, 84, 92–94
Erasmus (*see* Elmo, Saint)
Eustace, Saint, 93n
Expeditus, Saint, 190–192
Eyes, 1, 118–120

F

Fertility, 111, 113
Fourteen Holy Helpers, 92–93,
    108
Francis of Assisi, Saint, 108,
    186–189
Fugitives, 117
Future spouse, 23–26, 31–33,
    120–121

G

Gabriel, 5
Gandhi, Indira, 43
George, Saint, 93n, 122, 124–127
Gerard Majella, Saint, 104–106
Gertrude, Saint, 128–130
Giles, Saint, 93n
Glorious Mysteries, 199–200
Golden Legend, The, 9
Gossipmongers, 161, 162
Gregory of Tours, Saint, 63
Gregory the Great, Saint, 28,
    81–83

H

Hail Mary prayer, 32, 196
Handbook of Christian Feasts and
    Customs, The (Weiser), 12
Headaches, 97, 99, 100, 103
Health concerns, 6, 85–121
    arthritis and rheumatism,
        87–89
    chest pains, 100, 103
    childbirth, 111–113
    diseases of the breasts, 90–91
    eyes, 1, 118–120
    fertility, 111, 113
    headaches, 97, 99, 100,
        103
    pregnancy, 104–106
    stomach ailments, 92, 94
    throat ailments, 107–110
    toothache, 95–96
Hearth and home, 123–143

domestic pets, 131, 133–134,
    139, 140
house, garden, and domestic
    animals, problems with,
    131, 133–134
new home, 124, 126
selling home, 136, 138
vandalism, natural disasters,
    and the elements, 135, 137
vermin infestation, 128–130
violence, protection against,
    142–143
Heat, 179
Herod, King, 136
Holy water, 10
Hopeless causes, 1, 164–165

I

Ibor, Saint, 115
Insomnia, 63–65, 67
Interior Castle, The (Teresa of
    Avila), 102

J

James the Greater, Saint, 87–89
Jerome, Saint, 161
Jesus, 9, 44, 46, 57, 58, 87–88, 136,
    147, 164, 183
Joan of Arc, Saint, 54–56
John of the Cross, Saint, 65–67,
    136
John Paul II, Pope, 6
John the Apostle, 45, 87–88, 154
John the Baptist, Saint, 57–60,
    132, 183
Joseph, Saint, 1, 2, 102, 135–138,
    164, 197
Joyful Mysteries, 199–200
Judas Iscariot, 164, 165
Jude, Saint, 1, 142, 164–166, 197
Julian of Norwich, 46–48
Juno, Queen of Heaven, 35

K

Keats, John, 145

L

Lawrence, D.H., 145
Lawrence, Saint, 177–179
Liberata, Saint (*see* Wilgefortis,
 Saint)
Livrade, Saint (*see* Wilgefortis,
 Saint)
Lord's Prayer (Our Father), 196
Love and relationships, 17–41
 future spouse, 23–26, 31–33,
  120–121
 marital help, 40–41
 soul mates, 6, 17, 19, 21–22
 unwanted romantic partners,
  27, 29–30
Lucy, Saint, 1, 118–121
Luke, Saint (the Evangelist),
 31–33

M

Magic rituals, 11
Margaret of Antioch, Saint, 93n
Marital help, 40–41
Martin de Porres, Saint, 37–39
Martyrs, 5
Mary, mother of Jesus, 5, 32, 111,
 112, 151–153, 197–199
Mary Magdalen, Saint, 44–45, 101
Memorare, 150, 195
Michael the Archangel, Saint,
 142–143
Miracles, 6, 9, 14–15
Missing objects, 1, 6, 69–75
Money problems, 191–192
Monica, Saint, 40–41, 61
More, Sir Thomas, 29
Moses, 145
Mother Teresa, 51
Murdoch, Iris, 47
Musicians, 180–182

N

Natural disasters, 135, 137, 171,
 173
Nature, damage to, 186, 189

New home, 124, 126
Nicholas, Saint, 93n, 167–170
Nietzsche, Friedrich, 43
Novena, 197–198

P

Pagan rituals, 9–11
Pantaleon, Saint, 93n
Parking places, finding, 154,
 155
Patrick, Saint, 114, 115
Patron saints, 6
Paul, Saint, 31, 61, 98, 134
Performance anxiety, 180, 182
Pests, 6, 128–130
Peter, Saint, 91, 183
Pets, 131, 133–134, 139, 140
Phanourios, Saint, 74–75
Polycarp, Saint, 154
Prayers, 11, 194–200
 Apostles Creed, 195
 Confiteor (I Confess), 197
 Doxology (Glory Be), 194
 Hail Mary, 32, 196
 Lord's Prayer (Our Father),
  196
 Memorare, 150, 195
 Novena, 197–198
 Rosary beads, 198–200
 Sign of the Cross, 196
Pregnancy, 104–106
Procrastination, 191
Profession, choice of, 183, 184
Protestants, 11

R

Rainfall, 174–176
Real estate, 1, 6, 136, 138
Reformation, 9, 11
Regulus, Saint, 185
Relics, 10
Repentant sinners, 44–45
Revelations of Divine Love (Julian
 of Norwich), 46–47
Rheumatism, 87–89

Roch, Saint, 93*n*
Rosary beads, 198–200

S

Sacred and profane, 8–12
Sailors, 92–94
Saint Catherine's Monastery, 21,
22
Saint-Denis, abbey of, 98
St. John's wort, 59, 60
Saints
created by popular consensus,
4–5
defined, 3–4
patron, 6
relics, 10
Vatican canonization process,
4, 6, 14–15
Santa Claus, 167, 168
School stress, 77–83
Selling home, 136, 138
Seven Sleepers of Ephesus, 63–64
Shakespeare, William, 17, 125
Sign of the Cross, 196
Simon, Saint, 164
Sixtus, Saint, 177, 178
Smith, Sydney, 123
Solstice days, 10, 59, 140
Sorrowful Mysteries, 199–200
Soul mates, 6, 17, 19, 21–22
Spelunkers, 163
Spiritual Canticle (John of the
Cross), 65–67
Spouse, future, 23–26, 31–33,
120–121
Stephen, Saint, 131–134, 179
Stomach ailments, 92, 94
Story of a Soul, The (Thérèse of
Lisieux), 51
Stress, 46, 47, 49, 52–53
school, 77–83
Summa contra Gentiles (Thomas
Aquinas), 79
Summa Theologica (Thomas
Aquinas), 79

Supernatural powers, 9, 11
Superstitions, 8, 11, 12
Swithin, Saint, 174–176

T

Teresa of Avila, Saint, 66,
100–103, 136, 137
Thérèse of Lisieux, Saint, 42,
49–53
Thomas Aquinas, Saint, 76, 78–80
Thomas the Apostle, Saint, 132,
139–141
Thoreau, Henry David, 85
Throat, ailments of the, 107–110
Thunderstorms, 171, 173
Toothache, 95–96
Travel, 5, 145–155
True love, 34–37, 39
Twain, Mark, 69

U

Uncumber, Saint (*see* Wilgefortis,
Saint)
Unwanted romantic partners, 27,
29–30

V

Valentine, Saint, 34–36
Valerian, 180–181
Vandalism, 135, 137
Vermin infestation, 6, 128–130
Violence, protection against,
142–143
Vitus, Saint, 93*n*

W

Walsh, William, 152
Weather
heat, 179
rainfall, 174–176
thunderstorms, 171, 173
Weiser, Francis X., 12
Wilde, Oscar, 77
Wilgefortis, Saint, 27–30
Witches, 163

CPSIA information can be obtained
at www.ICGtesting.com
Printed in the USA
LVHW04s1727030718
582630LV00001B/6/P

9 780440 508656